# Reflect

### Discovering the Beauty, Worth, and Wonderfulness of You

## Vicki Courtney

B&H
PUBLISHING GROUP

Nashville, Tennessee

Published in association with the literary agency D.C. Jacobson & Associates, LLC, an
Author Management Company, www.dcjacobson.com, and Alive Communications, Inc.,
an Author Management Company, www.alivecommunications.com.

ISBN 978-1-4336-9175-1

Published by B&H Publishing Group
Nashville, Tennessee

Dewey Decimal Classification: Y155.2
GIRLS \ TEENAGERS \ PERFECTIONISM (PERSONALITY TRAIT)

Printed in June 2016 in Huizhou, Guangdong, China

1 2 3 4 5 6     20 19 18 17 16

# *Introduction*

If I could talk to teen girls about one thing and one thing only, it would be the topic of worth. The dictionary defines *worth* as "usefulness or importance, as to the world, to a person, or for a purpose." At the core of our being, we all want to feel useful and important. We want to know we matter in this great big world we live in. Unfortunately, most of us will look for worth in all the wrong places. I know this because doing so has been one of my greatest struggles.

When I reflect back on the biggest heartaches and struggles of my teen years, I can almost always trace it back to a misdefined sense of worth.

- When my self-esteem plummeted after failing to make the cheer squad in seventh, ninth, and eleventh grades: misdefined worth.

- When my self-esteem skyrocketed after making the cheer squad in eighth, tenth, and twelfth grades: misdefined worth.

- When my friends had boyfriends in ninth grade and I didn't, and I concluded I must be undesirable: misdefined worth.

- When I had severe acne in high school and avoided swim parties because my makeup might wash off: misdefined worth.

- When I engaged in fad starvation diets to stay thin and ended up with an eating disorder: misdefined worth.

- When I drank alcohol with my friends in order to fit in and be cool: misdefined worth.

- When I weighed myself several times a day to make sure I hadn't gained a single pound: misdefined worth.

- When I obsessed over owning name-brand clothes and accessories in order to impress my peers: misdefined worth.

- When I had sex with my high-school boyfriend because I thought that's what I had to do to keep him: misdefined worth.

And the list goes on and on. But here's the deal about misdefined worth: if you don't reject the lies you've come to believe, and if you never discover where your true worth comes from, you will carry that same warped formula into your adult years. Trust me, the fallout will be immense.

So, what is the lie most girls today believe when it comes to their self-worth and where it can be found? Look at this simple mathematical formula:

Worth = What you look like + What you do + What others think

Fortunately, God has a different formula when it comes to worth:

Worth = Who you are

## Which formula have you come to believe?

In *Reflect*, we are going to talk about your worth. We are going to unpack the lies and, more importantly, talk about the truth. My prayer is that by the time you turn the last page of this book, you will vow to reject the lies because you know exactly where true worth can be found.

Your worth crusader,

### Vicki Courtney

*As you read, you'll find several QR codes with questions next to them. Using any QR reader app, scan the codes to connect to videos of teen girls giving their answers to the questions. How do their answers compare to yours?*

*When you see a QR code like this, scan it!*

Scan for Video Answers!

# About the Writers . . .

***Vicki Courtney*** is a speaker and best-selling author of numerous books and Bible studies. She began writing about the culture's influence on tween and teen girls in 2003 and has a passion to see girls and women of all ages find their worth in Christ. Vicki is married to Keith, and they live in Austin, Texas. They are parents to three grown children, who are all married and live nearby. Vicki enjoys spending time at the lake, hanging out with her family, and spoiling her grandchildren rotten. More information about Vicki can be found at VickiCourtney.com.

***Ali Claxton*** is a freelance writer, editor, Bible study leader, mentor, storyteller, coffee drinker, aspiring novelist, and avid reader. She has a marketing degree and an MBA from Mississippi State University and is currently pursuing a master's degree in theological studies from the Southern Baptist Theological Seminary. She has served in girls' ministry for over a decade and loves seeing God move in the lives of teenagers.

***Pam Gibbs*** is a writer, editor, speaker, youth minister, and amateur archer, but her favorite titles are wife and mom. She is a graduate of Southwestern Baptist Theological Seminary and leads teens at her church. When she's not hanging out with her tween daughter and teacher/coach husband, you'll find her curled up with a good mystery book and some dark chocolate.

***Tami Overhauser*** is a blogger who writes about parenting, real life, and a really big God. She is a wife and busy mom to four children. Tami enjoys spending time with family (especially at the beach!), cooking, running, and laughing. More information about Tami can be found on her blog, RaisingAdam.com.

***Ashley Anderson*** works for Young Life and leads the college women's ministry at the University of Texas. She is a writer and speaker who is passionate about empowering women with the Word of God. Ashley is married to Micah, and they have a daughter, Nora. They live in Austin, Texas, in a home they renovated together.

***Rachel Prochnow*** is the founder of Radically Radiant Ministries, which is devoted to helping girls understand their immeasurable worth as daughters of the King. To learn more about Rachel and Radically Radiant Ministries, go to radicallyradiant.com.

***Whitney Prosperi*** has a heart for girls and girls' ministry. She is the author of *Life Style: Real Perspectives from Radical Women in the Bible*, a twelve-week Bible study for middle and high school girls, as well as *Girls Ministry 101*, published by Youth Specialties. She lives in Tyler, Texas, with her husband, Randy, and daughters, Annabelle and Libby.

Rebecca,

I can't believe how fast you've grown up! It seems like yesterday when we were playing with toys, watching Hermie + Wormie and experiencing your first Disney adventure. You've grown into a precious young woman — smart and determined, passionate and talented. I am proud to be your aunt. Every time I write for teenage girls, I pray for words that encourage and point to the Source of our hope and value. This book is filled with challenging thoughts from people I admire. I had the privilege of writing several articles/devotions and coordinating the project as we determined what would be included. I hope you will be encouraged and reminded of your infinite value in Christ as you read these pages.

Much love,
Aunt Alicia

# Contents

Mirror, Mirror . . . . . . . . . . . . . . . . . 9

That Thing You Do . . . . . . . . . 61

Get More Likes . . . . . . . . . . . . . . 109

The Truth of the Matter . . 157

# Mirror, Mirror

# The Truth About Charm

*by Vicki Courtney*

Not long ago my publicist forwarded me an e-mail she had received from the producer of a radio show. I had done an interview for his show the day before on the subject of Internet safety. The e-mail said, "Vicki was absolutely charming, and we plan to have her on the show again in the future." I have to admit that I smiled when I read the word *charming*. What a great word! Who doesn't want to be considered charming? The dictionary defines *charm* as "a quality that attracts and pleases."[1] So how does one obtain the elusive quality of charm? And where, exactly, does it fit in our Christian walk? Is charm on God's list of approved qualities?

I have a collection of vintage *Seventeen* magazines and may have stumbled upon the secret to charm while thumbing through an issue from October 1949. An article by a "noted beauty authority" addressed the three fundamentals of charm. Get ready to laugh.

## The Three Fundamentals of Charm in 1949

- Vigorous aliveness
- Appealing good looks
- Ability to meet life gaily

Get ready to laugh even more. The author went on to stress the importance of "physical well-being" as the secret to the three fundamentals of charm, summing it up by saying, "You can't be gay [I swear it says this], you can't be vigorous, and you can't look your best if you're not in good condition." That advice may have been helpful in 1949, but I'm thinking it's a bit outdated for the average teen girl today.

So what exactly does God say about charm? Does the Bible even address it? Amazingly, it does. Proverbs 31:30 says, "Charm is deceptive, and beauty is fleeting; but a woman who fears the Lord will be praised." The original Hebrew word for *deceptive* in the verse is *sheqer*, and it means "an untruth" or "a sham."[2] When I think of the word *sham*, I think of an e-mail I just got this morning from a friend. It included a touching story and then, at the end, it said that if I didn't forward it to ten friends right away, something bad might happen to me. Hmm. I deleted the e-mail and discounted it as a sham.

A sham is not worth my time. I have more important matters to deal with than to go through my address book in order to play along with a silly superstition. Equally, the pursuit of charm is not worth my time. Why invest in something that bids for the attention of man when I should care more about pleasing my heavenly Father?

The second part of Proverbs 31:30 is clear on what makes God's list when it comes to admirable qualities: "A woman who fears the Lord will be praised." So what in the world does it mean to "fear the Lord"? When I hear the word *fear*, I think of knee-knocking, teeth-chattering, I-just-saw-a-ghost kind of fear. Is God talking about that kind of fear? Does He want us to be afraid of Him? The "fear" that God speaks of is quite different. It is an awe and reverence for Him—an awesome respect. One Bible dictionary describes fear of the Lord as:

- dreading God's displeasure
- desiring God's favor
- revering God's holiness
- submitting cheerfully to God's will
- being grateful for God's benefits
- worshipping God sincerely
- obeying God's commandments[3]

Let's break down these qualities to understand what is involved in fearing the Lord. This is an opportunity for you to self-assess and to ask yourself where you stand in regard to each characteristic.

***Do you dread God's displeasure?*** You know that feeling you get when one of your parents is disappointed about something you have done? Would it concern you if you knew God was displeased with your actions? Would it motivate you to avoid displeasing Him?

***Do you desire God's favor?*** Are you more concerned with winning the favor of man or God? Sadly, most Christians seem more concerned with being people-pleasers than God-pleasers.

***Do you revere God's holiness?*** Do you use the name of the Lord in vain or remain silent when others do? Or do you cringe when you hear someone blaspheming His holy name? The culture may find it cute to refer to Jesus as a "homeboy," but you know better. Someone who dies for sinners deserves to be called Savior.

***Do you submit cheerfully to God's will?*** Are you committed to seeking out God's will by reading the Bible and praying consistently? When you know what God wants you to do in a situation, do you do it even if it's not the popular thing to do?

***Are you grateful for God's benefits?*** Do you regularly thank Him for all He has done for you? Or do you focus more in your prayer time on what you would like Him to do for you? Do you face life with an attitude that says the glass is half-full rather than half-empty? The truth is, with God at the center, the glass overflows.

***Do you sincerely worship God?*** Do you recognize that worship is more than a song offered to God in a church service? Do you see worship as an attitude of the heart that is constantly aware that God is God and we are not?

***Do you obey God's commandments?*** Do you filter decisions through the commandments God set forth in the Bible? Has it become second nature for you to obey first and ask questions later?

So how did you do? Don't beat yourself up if you fall short. Remember, we are works in progress when it comes to spiritual maturity. The truth is, we all have room for improvement when it comes to fearing the Lord. If you are struggling to fear Him, start by praying and sharing your struggle with God. Ask Him to help you focus your attention on learning what it means to fear Him. And then work on the list above by putting your fear of the Lord into practice.

Remember wise King Solomon in the Old Testament? At God's prompting he wrote the beautiful book of Ecclesiastes. He was best known for possessing great wisdom. He had personally reaped the benefits of wealth, knowledge, and power, yet he continued to question the meaning of life throughout his years. At the end of Ecclesiastes, he concludes with a profound statement. Let me sum it up for you: when all is said and done, on the day you stand before your Maker, charm will be powerless on the One who matters most.

Has anyone ever called you "charming"? If so, what were the circumstances, and how did it make you feel?

If the Bible tells us that "charm is deceptive and beauty is fleeting," why do you think so many girls still chase after charm and beauty?

When you read over the qualities of what it means to "fear the Lord," which ones need development?

Overall, would you say that you show a healthy awe and reverence for God?

Would others close to you say that you are more focused on beauty and charm or fearing the Lord?

***Sources:***

1. *Merriam-Webster Online*, s.v. "charm," http://www.merriam-webster.com/dictionary/charm.

2. James Strong, *The New Strong's Concise Dictionary of the Words in the Greek Testament and the Hebrew Bible*, s.v. "deceptive," (Bellingham, WA: Logos, 2009).

3. Merrill F. Unger, *The New Unger's Bible Dictionary* (Chicago: Moody, 2006).

# PRETTY PACKAGING

*by Vicki Courtney*

Have you ever been lured in by pretty packaging? Product manufacturers who aim for successful sales know the importance of packaging. Furthermore, they know that consumers make as much as 70 percent of their buying decisions in the store and can face up to a hundred thousand items that bid for their attention. Whether it's a pack of gum, a tube of toothpaste, or a bag of chips, you can bet that countless dollars and hours have been invested into analyzing everything from the target audience to color palettes and shelf placement. The end goal, of course, is for the product to stand out and, above all, get picked up by the consumer and scanned at the checkout.

Now, what if I told you that you are also a product? Your brand managers work around the clock to make sure you know exactly what it will take to get noticed. If you are to catch the eye of your target audience, the packaging must be perfect. And by perfect, I mean *flawless*. By the time you celebrate your twelfth birthday, you will have seen an estimated 77,546 commercials. Add to

*Charm is deceptive and beauty is fleeting, but a woman who fears the LORD will be praised. —Proverbs 31:30*

that the images you see daily from magazines, billboards, and the Internet—and by the time you blow out sixteen candles, you will be crystal clear of your role as defined by our shallow culture.

Over and over again you will be told to lose weight, tone up, dress provocatively, and flaunt it. Pure and simple, you are an object for viewing pleasure. You are bidding for male attention among a sea of contenders, and your target audience is picky. They, too, have been inundated with images of picture-perfect women. They have zero tolerance for flat chests, chunky thighs, cellulite, blemishes, split ends, or facial wrinkles. Why should any man settle for less than a Photoshop best? They have been led to believe that airbrushed images are the standard of beauty, and that such beauty is easily attainable.

So, how does it feel to be treated like a product? Are you mad? You should be! You are more than the sum of your parts, so don't buy into the culture's lie. Ninety-three percent of girls and young women report feeling anxiety or stress about some aspect of their looks when getting ready in the morning. More than three-quarters of girls and young women admit to partaking in unhealthy activities when they feel insecure about their bodies. Fifty-eight percent of girls describe

themselves in negative terms, including words like *disgusting* and *ugly*, when feeling bad about themselves. Nearly four out of ten engage in unhealthy eating behaviors, such as anorexia or bulimia. If you conform your identity to the culture's narrow definition of beauty, you can be sure that it will permeate every corner of your life.

Believe it or not, it hasn't always been this way. If you were to sneak a peek into the average teenage girl's diary from over a century ago, you would find very little, if any, preoccupation with outer appearance. One author researched girls' diaries and journals from the late 1800s to early 1900s to track the shift in attitudes regarding appearance. She found that "before World War I, girls rarely mentioned their bodies in terms of strategies for self-improvement or struggles for personal identity." She stated, "When girls in the nineteenth century thought about ways to improve themselves, they almost always focused on their internal character and how it was reflected in outward behavior. In 1882, the personal agenda of an adolescent diarist read: 'Resolved, not to talk about myself or feelings. To think before speaking. To work seriously. To be self-restrained in conversation and actions. Not to let my thoughts wander. To be dignified. Interest myself more in others.'"[1]

A century ago, beauty was defined by virtue rather than vanity. My, how times have changed (and not necessarily for the better!). Girls from the nineteenth century were likely raised on that biblical wisdom of Proverbs 31:30, which counsels, "Charm is deceptive and beauty is fleeting, but a woman who fears the LORD will be praised." How exactly did this shift from virtue to vanity occur? Believe it or not, your bathroom mirror is partially to blame. The same author who examined girls' diaries from over a century ago stated, "When the mirror became a staple of the American middle-class home at the end of the nineteenth century, attention to adolescent acne escalated, as did sales of products for the face." She further noted that "mirrors play a critical role in the way American girls have assessed their own faces and figures."[2]

With mirrors, women were able to scrutinize and compare their features with the women they saw in movies and magazines—not to mention one another. In the 1920s, American women began to take an interest in cosmetics. Searching for facial powders, rouge, lipstick, and even eyelash curlers, ladies flocked to the local drugstores to stock up on beauty novelties. Shortly thereafter, home scales became available, and managing weight became a preoccupation among young women. Until then, the only place a young woman could weigh herself was the drugstore or county fair!

While it's not possible to do away with mirrors or scales and revert back to the late 1800s, it is possible to do away with our unhealthy attitudes about beauty. There is nothing wrong with paying attention to our appearance, but if it becomes more important than improving our heart, we've bought into the lie at some level.

What is your definition of beauty?

***Sources:***
1. Quoted in Joan Jacobs Brumberg, *The Body Project: An Intimate History of American Girls* (New York: Vintage, 1998), xxi.
2. Ibid., 64–66.

*Q. How do you think the world defines beauty?*

Scan for Video Answers!

# Confessions of a Beauty Queen

*by Rachel Prochnow*

Tears brimmed in her light green eyes and wet her long, dark lashes. Blonde hair cascaded in perfectly formed curls down her back. She gazed in the mirror.

She hated what she saw.

When others looked at her, they saw the prom queen, the girl with the perfect boyfriend, the star athlete, the state pageant winner, the girl who never lost, the girl everyone wanted for a best friend, the girl who could glide into a room and turn every eye.

She saw herself differently.

All she saw were flaws. She was confident, yes, but it was a show. She was playing a role—a role she had been cast into long ago: the beauty queen. And she played it flawlessly.

Yet behind the curtain, she was terrified. Terrified of what people would think of her if they saw her stripped clean of the makeup, the hairspray, the outer shell. She wouldn't allow anyone to get too close. If they did, they might see the real her—the girl behind the pageant persona.

That girl was me.

For a long time, I found my worth and identity in how I looked or how others perceived me. I wanted to be seen as the girl who was beautiful and had it all together. That desire dictated many things I did. I never left the house without a full face of makeup or my hair perfectly curled. I relished the compliments related to my appearance. I desperately wanted people to think I was beautiful.

But it was exhausting.

No matter how I looked or how thin I got, I never felt adequate. At the height of my insecurity, I was terrified to let my boyfriend see me without makeup because I thought he might not love me if he knew what I actually looked like. Our society puts an enormous amount of pressure on girls to look perfect all the time. Everywhere we go, we are bombarded with airbrushed and Photoshopped models. We are told at an early age how a beautiful woman "should" look. Even the dolls we play with as six-year-olds have unrealistic and unattainable body types. What I am about to say is the opposite of everything that has been impressed upon you by your peers and the media.

Beauty is not everything.

Take it from someone who has tried to find her worth in external appearance: you will never be happy if you place more importance on what's on the outside than what's on the inside. True beauty resides in the heart. Ephesians 5:1 commands, "Therefore be imitators of God as dear children" (NKJV). Do you want to be beautiful? Try to be more like Christ! Walk in His love and His peace. Read the Word of God. Look for ways to serve those around you. A beautiful soul is of far greater value than a beautiful face.

True beauty doesn't come from a flawless complexion or a number on the scale. True beauty comes with reflecting Christ and showing His love to others. It took me a long time to understand that.

Here are some questions to ponder: When people look at your life, do they see Christ? Is your love for God one of the first things people learn about you? How do you show those around you Christ's love? When was the last time you did a random act of kindness?

As daughters of the King, we have a higher calling. We are called to reflect Him in all we do. That means allowing His perfect love to shine through our actions. Our identity is rooted in Christ. In Him, we are beautiful.

You have immeasurable worth because of what Christ has done for you.

Do you believe it?

*You have immeasurable worth because of what Christ has done for you.*

# Quiz: What's Beautiful to You?

*by Ali Claxton*

Take a moment to answer the following questions.

1. **What do you notice first about people when they walk in the room?**

A. Smile

B. Hair

C. Clothes

D. The way they carry themselves

2. **What is your favorite season of the year?**

A. Summer: sunshine, blue skies, bright colors

B. Fall: changing scenery, autumn colors, falling leaves

C. Winter: layers of clothes, snow, Christmas colors

D. Spring: brilliant colors, rainy days, new beginnings

3. **What kind of art captures your attention?**

A. Paintings of nature

B. Photography

C. Abstract art

D. Images of people

4. **When you step inside someone's home, what's the first thing you notice?**

A. Furniture

B. Color scheme

C. Pictures

D. Collectibles or trinkets

5. **When you travel to new places, what do you look forward to seeing most?**

A. Scenic views

B. Fun shops and restaurants

C. Historical sites

D. People

6. **Which vacation destination would you choose?**

A. Mountains

B. Beach

C. Fancy hotel

D. Camping in a national park

7. **Which outfit makes you feel the most beautiful?**

A. Elegant dress with heels

B. Cute summer dress with sandals

C. Jeans and colorful sweater with boots

D. Shorts and fun T-shirt with tennis shoes

There's no right or wrong answer to these questions. This quiz isn't a test of your knowledge or an opinion poll to see which option is more popular. It's based on your individual preferences—what you like, what captures your attention, what moves you. If you and a roomful of friends all took this same quiz, many of your answers would differ. That's because you are different people and you like different things. You see the world with your own unique outlook, and you define beauty based on that perspective.

Our capacity for seeing beauty in the world around us expands as we grow and experience new things. Our ability to see beauty in ourselves and others deepens as we recognize the infinite value we've been created with.

There's beauty all around you if you choose to see it.

Can you see it when you look in the mirror?

Do you recognize it in others?

# BEAUTY BY THE BOOK

*by Vicki Courtney*

*I praise you because I am fearfully and wonderfully made; your works are wonderful, I know that full well. —Psalm 139:14 NIV*

**What it means:** You are created in the image of God, and God doesn't make junk! Every person is unique and different, like a snowflake. No two are the same. God sees you as a masterpiece, and when you look in the mirror, He wants you to "know that full well." Try this beauty tip: every morning when you look in the mirror, say Psalm 139:14 and smile. You might even tape the verse up on your mirror as a reminder!

*But the LORD said to Samuel, "Do not consider his appearance or his height, for I have rejected him. The LORD does not look at the things people look at. People look at the outward appearance, but the LORD looks at the heart." —1 Samuel 16:7 NIV*

**What it means:** The world focuses on what people look like on the outside. God focuses on what people look like on the inside. Do you put more time and effort into being pretty on the outside or the inside? As you get older, you will meet Christian girls who spend more time trying to find the perfect outfit, get the perfect tan, find the perfect lip gloss, and have the perfect body. While there's nothing wrong with wanting to look pretty, we need to make sure it's in balance. God would rather see us work on becoming drop-dead gorgeous on the inside. You know, the kind of girl who talks to Him on a regular basis in prayer and reads her Bible.

*Charm is deceptive and beauty is fleeting, but a woman who fears the LORD will be praised.* —Proverbs 31:30

**What it means:** Beauty fades with age, so if you are more concerned with your outer appearance, you will be unhappy when the wrinkles come and the number on the scale goes up. In fact, did you know that your body may show the first signs of aging as early as age twenty? Physical beauty will fade, but character remains. That is why God wants us to "fear" Him. He wants us to be in awe of Him and all He has done. Let's pretend you could stand two girls next to each other: one is Miss Teen USA, whose beauty is limited to the physical, and the other young lady is average-looking but loves the Lord more than anything. The one who loves God is the more beautiful girl His eyes.

*Your beauty should not come from outward adornment, such as elaborate hairstyles and the wearing of gold jewelry or fine clothes. Rather, it should be that of your inner self, the unfading beauty of a gentle and quiet spirit, which is of great worth in God's sight.* —1 Peter 3:3–4 NIV

**What it means:** This does not mean it's wrong to braid your hair or wear nice clothes and jewelry. The verse was written to warn women within the church not to follow the customs of some pagan women who, during that time period, spent hours and hours working on their hair, makeup, and outfits. God would rather see women working on becoming beautiful on the inside—the kind of beauty that lasts forever.

*The training of the body has a limited benefit, but godliness is beneficial in every way, since it holds promise for the present life and also for the life to come.* —1 Timothy 4:8

**What it means:** Exercising and staying in shape is a good thing, but God expects us to stay in shape spiritually by reading our Bibles, praying, and going to church on a regular basis. In other words, there will be plenty of people who put their time and effort into staying in shape physically, but they could be out of shape spiritually. If they don't know Jesus Christ, their perfect bodies won't get them through the gates of heaven.

# Accepting Your God-Given Body Shape

*by Vicki Courtney*

On a recent afternoon while shopping with my daughter, I waited outside her dressing room while she tried on some jeans. In the dressing room next to her, a young lady yelled out to her friend, "Oh-em-gee! I am so fat! I can't fit into these size zeros. Will you go get me a size two?" Seriously, I wanted to crawl under the door of that fitting room and feed the girl a cheeseburger. I prayed my daughter had ignored the whole exchange, but chances are, she heard it.

Such words put chinks in the armor of the body image battle that wages war within the souls of most women, young and old alike. Rather than logically deduce that statements like the one above are products of our culture's narrow definition of beauty, most girls within hearing range will instead glance at themselves in the mirror and feel disgust and shame.

One survey found that by age thirteen, 53 percent of American girls are unhappy with their bodies; and by age seventeen, 78 percent are dissatisfied. If we are to counter the culture's lies regarding body image, we must go first to the root of the problem and address body shape. I am talking about the God-given body shape you are born with, rather than the hourglass ideal the media insists you should have.

Over and over again you will be exposed to images of models whose bodies are not representative of the majority of women. One study found that the hourglass figure is the least dominant shape of women, having made up only 8 percent of the 6,318 US women who were scanned for the study. In fact, 46 percent of women were found to have more of a rectangle shape, 21 percent were spoon-shaped, and 14 percent were shaped more like an inverted triangle. The study further found that the hourglass shape almost does not exist in women larger than a size eight.

25

Keep in mind that the average American teen girl is 5 feet, 3.8 inches tall and weighs 134.5 pounds. Yet the garment industry assumes that the hourglass figure is the dominant shape of American women and designs their clothing to fit that shape. As a result, many girls are unable to find clothes designed to fit them. Remember that the next time you see a Victoria's Secret model, and your friends start hopping on the thigh-gap bandwagon. A model's body shape represents a tiny percentage of the female population, and most of them have been airbrushed beyond recognition anyway! It's a losing battle.

Geometry lesson aside, let's imagine a world without pre-manufactured clothing sizes. A century ago, clothes were often made at home. In *The Body Project*, Joan Jacobs Brumberg notes, "In general, mass-produced clothing fostered autonomy in girls because it took matters of style and taste outside the dominion of the mother, who had traditionally made and supervised a girl's wardrobe . . . So long as clothing was made at home, the dimensions of the garment could be adjusted to the particular body intended to wear it. But with store-bought clothes, the body had to fit instantaneously into standard sizes that were constructed from a pattern representing a norm."[1]

I am certainly not suggesting you give up shopping and ask your mother to sew your clothes. (Can you even imagine?!) But next time you find yourself in a dressing room battle, cut yourself some slack . . . and remember that standardized clothes are designed to fit a body shape that is not common anyway. And if you have some spare time on your hands, contact that designer and make an appeal for a change.

When we wish to look like someone else, in a sense we are implying that God made a mistake when He created us. In Romans 9:20, the apostle Paul says, "Who are you, a human being, to talk back to God? 'Shall what is formed say to the one who formed it, "Why did you make me like this?"'" (NIV). Quit arguing with God and learn to appreciate His beautiful handiwork.

I wish I could go back and tell my younger self these truths. I know firsthand the fallout from believing the perfect-body-image lies. I suffered from an eating disorder in my teen and college years, and I regret the time I wasted trying to achieve a weight and shape that was extremely unhealthy and impossible to maintain because God never intended me to be that thin. It wasn't until many years later that I learned to love and appreciate the shape God has given me. It wasn't easy, and I had to work hard to replace the lies I had come to believe with constant reminders of God's truth. When I was tempted to grumble at my reflection in the mirror, I had to catch myself and make a concentrated effort to thank God for the amazing body He gave me.

What if you decided today to accept your God-given body shape and be content with it? Rather than focusing on an impossible ideal that will leave you forever dissatisfied with your reflection, make it your goal to focus instead on being healthy. If you want to look your best, then eat right and exercise. Come up with a plan to look like the best possible you rather than the best possible someone else. Make friends with your body shape. While you're at it, tell God thanks when you catch a reflection of yourself in the mirror.

*Source:*

1. Joan Jacobs Brumberg, *The Body Project: An Intimate History of American Girls* (New York: Vintage, 1998), 107.

*Q. How do you think God defines beauty?*

Scan for Video Answers!

# NOT YOUR GRANDMA'S WORLD!

*by Vicki Courtney*

Ever wonder what it was like when your grandma was a teenager?

We know that teenagers growing up in the 1940s through the 1960s didn't have cable, computers, or cell phones. There were some things in common, such as boys, school, and parents. Other than that, it was a much different world.

Without texting, social media, or Netflix, how in the world did they fill their days?

Would you believe that they had fashion magazines? In fact, *Seventeen* was actually launched in 1944. It is amazing to compare the articles, ads, and pictures from the early issues of that magazine to the current versions of the same teen magazine. Flipping through some of the old magazines gives us a glimpse of what life was like for the average teenage girl.

Did you know that issues of *Seventeen Magazine* from 1945 to 1960 included an average of ten ads for sterling silver flatware, diamond engagement rings, and china? Clearly, marriage and family were on the mind of the average teenage girl in Grandma's day.

What about today? Well, you can forget about the pro-marriage ads. In fact, I couldn't find any hint or mention of marriage as a future option in today's teen magazines.

What about the relationships between teenage girls and guys in the 1940s to 1960s?

Again, the images in ads and articles hint at what it was like in Grandma's day. Notice the obvious respect the guys have for the girls in the pictures below.

In this *Seventeen* cover from 1950, the young man is reading poetry to a young woman. Yeah, as if that happens a lot today!

The teen fashion magazines of today are full of images of guys and girls with their hands all over each other. In fact, most pictures show the girls as the aggressors or the ones in charge. Each magazine contains countless images of girls sitting on guys' laps or straddling them and sporting facial expressions loaded with attitude.

What about the topics of interest for the average teen girl in Grandma's day? Many articles dealt with art, music, friendship, faith, and family. In the articles that addressed parents, there was always encouragement to obey and respect parents, whereas many of today's articles in the teen magazines treat parents like clueless idiots who are out to sabotage their daughters' lives. As for common topics of interest in today's magazines, Grandma would be shocked to find articles on oral sex, homosexuality, birth control, and cross-dressing teens. Wow, things sure have changed.

The teen magazines from Grandma's day did not have articles like "22 Jeans That Scream 'Nice Butt,'" "Swimsuit Tops That Tease and Please," and "How to Be a Guy Magnet." So, if Grandma didn't have advice on how to be a guy magnet or what to wear to make guys drool, how in the world did she ever manage to snag Grandpa? Surely she

didn't attract him with her mind or heart—that just wouldn't be right, would it?

Teenage girls in Grandma's day may not have had smartphones or current technology, but they generally had faith and a love for family and were respected by the guys they knew. At first glance, it may seem like they were missing out on a lot, but if you ask me, when it comes to the important things in life, maybe we're the ones missing out.

# Back in The Day

THE LADIES' HOME JOURNAL, APRIL 1890

## How to Act Before the Camera: Advice from a Veteran Photographer

*A. Bogardus*

Women do, and should, study to be graceful in bearing at all times, and this accomplishment will come in good stead when having a picture made.

As to impression: Look as you always do. The attempt to put on an extraordinary expression for the occasion has spoiled many a picture. Remember, the photographer is not to make your looks; he is to copy your looks. He will endeavor to execute it to the best advantage; but it must be as you are, and not as you would like to be. I once made the pictures of one of our venerable judges and his wife. The proofs of the judge were satisfactory, but the wife thought her looks too old. The judge said, "Mother, it is very perfect; if you had expected a pretty picture you should have commenced thirty years ago."

I cannot conclude these few words of advice to women, when sitting for their portraits, better than by saying briefly:

Dress simply and becomingly
Act in your natural manner
Be yourself

Then, if the operator be a good one, you will get a satisfactory picture.

# The Story Behind the Bikini

*by Pam Gibbs*

It happens every year. Summertime rolls around, and it's time to buy a new bathing suit. You know it's coming—the swimsuit argument with your mom.

**Mom:** The top is too small. The bottoms are barely there. It shows too much skin.

**You:** All the girls wear swimsuits like this! What's wrong with a bikini? I can't find anything else I like!

Sound familiar? Millions of moms, dads, and daughters get caught up in a heated argument over these polarizing pieces of clothing. You may think this is the first generation to battle over a bikini, but this struggle over the string bikini has been an ongoing war for a century.

## A Little History

Do you know where the bikini came from? Probably not. It wasn't introduced until the 1940s. In the early 1900s, women wouldn't dare bare their derrieres at the beach. They would step into a "bathing machine"—a tiny, mobile dressing room on wheels. Once inside, they would get into their bathing suits (think a very conservative jumper). Then horses (or humans) pulled the cart into the water. The women would walk out on the sea's side so they could get into the water without being seen from the shore. The culture was so modest back then that a woman was arrested on the beach in Australia in 1907 for wearing a tight-fitting bathing suit that—get this—showed her arms and legs.

When the 1940s rolled around, an early version of the bikini was introduced. It exposed a sliver of skin between the top and bottom pieces—like a modest tankini—but the bottoms were more like leggings.

## The Bikini Is Born

Bikinis didn't originate in America. They came from France and were introduced by two different designers, each with his own prototype. One designer, Jacques Helm, called his creation the "Atome" (French for "atom") in honor of the recently discovered atom—connecting the size of the atom with the size of the bathing suit! Around the same time, Louis Reard created an even smaller two-piece creation and called it a "bikini." It was named after the Bikini Atoll, where the US had begun testing the atomic bomb. He wanted his suit to be as memorable and shocking as an atomic bomb. It was so scandalous that French fashion models refused to wear it, and Reard had to hire a stripper to model it in public. Later, he bragged that his bikini was so small it could be pulled through a wedding ring. The people of Europe were outraged, and the bikini was banned on Italian and Spanish beaches for years.

Even into the late 1950s, Americans didn't take to the European-style, scandalous swimsuit. A magazine called *Modern Girl* announced in 1957: "It is hardly necessary to waste words over the so-called bikini since it is inconceivable that any girl with tact and decency would ever wear such a thing."[1] Fast-forward fifty-plus years, and you'd be hard-pressed to find a teenage girl who doesn't own a bikini. Annual two-piece bathing suit sales in the US topped *eight billion dollars* last year alone.[2]

I'm certainly not suggesting that you wear a wetsuit the next time you go for a swim, but I think it's helpful for girls to stop and consider how the fashions of the day came to be. More importantly, we should consider how they measure up against truths in the Bible. Many other choices and activities that were once considered scandalous—sex outside of marriage, debt, abortion, homosexual marriage, euthanasia, cheating, lying, drug and alcohol abuse—are now accepted by mainstream culture. It reminds me of something my grandmother used to say: "Just because you *can*, doesn't mean you *should*."

Here's the truth for believers, though: Christ has called us to be *counter*cultural. We should live *differently* from the non-Christians around us. Remember what Jesus said in the Sermon on the Mount?

"You are the salt of the earth. But if the salt loses its saltiness, how can it be made salty again? It is no longer good for anything, except to be thrown out and trampled underfoot. You are the light of the world. A town built on a hill cannot be hidden. Neither do people light a lamp and put it under a bowl. Instead they put it on its stand, and it gives light to everyone in the house. In the same way, let your light shine before others, that they may see your good deeds and glorify your Father in heaven" (Matthew 5:13–16 NIV).

Salt doesn't taste like the food it flavors but enhances the food itself. Light changes the darkness around it. A believer's life shouldn't look like an unbeliever's. When you're in a dressing room with a stack of swimwear, take a second to think about what you want your life to look like. As a Christian teen, God has called you to "shine among them like stars in the sky" (Philippians 2:15 NIV). You can't shine like a star if your life looks just like everyone else's.

## Ask Yourself . . .

This truth is relevant whether you're swimsuit shopping, choosing a movie to watch, or texting with your friends. If we as believers are called to glorify God in whatever we do, then we need to ask ourselves a really tough question when making any choice: *Would this honor or dishonor God?*

The next time you put on that swimsuit, consider why you are wearing it. If your motivation isn't in step with the Word of God and the calling to glorify Him, put something else on. (This applies to the rest of your closet, too!) It's supposed to be all about Him—not all about you.

*Sources:*

1. Julia Turner, "A Brief History of the Bikini," Slate.com, last modified July 3, 2015, http://www.slate.com/articles/life/fashion/2013/07/history_of_the_bikini_how_it_came_to_america.html.

2. "Swimwear Industry Statistic," *Statistic Brain Research Institute*, http://www.statisticbrain.com/swimwear-industry-statistics.

# THE SEXY CRAZE

*by Vicki Courtney*

It's everywhere you look. The word *sexy* is so overused, I'm not even sure what it means anymore. Sexy jeans. Sexy lips. Sexy swimsuits. Sexy handbags. Can a purse be sexy? Give me a break! So what's up with the sexy craze? And more importantly, why do we care?

When I looked up the word *sexy* in the dictionary, I found two definitions. One says this: "arousing or tending to arouse sexual desire or interest." The slang definition is: "highly appealing or interesting; attractive."[1] I'm going to go out on a limb here and assume that in the majority of cases the word is used as slang and the latter definition applies. Show me a single handbag that makes a guy want to have sex with you, and I might change my mind. I think you get my point.

So what's wrong, then, with Christian girls buying into the "be sexy" message? It boils down to a question of motives. For some girls, *sexy* is not about looking attractive or appealing, which the slang term implies; *sexy* is about arousing the opposite sex. For these girls, is the final goal to have sex with the intended target or just to be noticed? Is their goal to attract negative attention? Girls, don't be fooled by the messages of this sex-crazed culture—you don't have to play this game to get guys to notice you.

For many girls your age, the sincere motive is to look attractive, not so much sexy. I'd be lying if I told you it isn't nice to be noticed every once in a while. If we're honest, we can all admit to wanting to turn a few heads. What girl doesn't remember the compliments she's received from guys? Especially if they came from that cute guy you happen to like. Is it really a sin to look attractive? No, it's not. In fact, God wants you to take care of yourself. Remember, your body is the temple of the Holy Spirit, and we should take pride in His temple. It drives me crazy when Christians imply that women should seek to look plain and sometimes even frumpy when decorating His temple. I like to look attractive, and I'm not afraid to admit it.

Looking attractive is not a sin, but it does become a sin if your motive is to arouse the opposite sex. It becomes a sin if the end result would disgrace rather than compliment God's temple. It becomes a sin if you care more about what others will think rather than what God thinks. In the end, *sexy* just doesn't seem like a word that God would want others to use when describing the very residence in which His Spirit resides.

**Source:**
1. *The American Heritage Dictionary of the English Language*, Fourth Edition, s.v. "sexy," (New York: Houghton Mifflin, 2000).

# NEVER EVER

*Never ever define your worth by:*

- *your reflection in the mirror*

- *a number on the scale*

- *your jean size*

- *a clear complexion*

- *a bra size*

- *the number of compliments you get on your appearance*

- *how you look in a swimsuit*

- *washboard abs*

- *a thigh-gap*

- *how much attention you get from guys*

- *clean eating and healthy nutrition*

- *being labeled "sexy"*

- *comparing yourself to airbrushed models*

*You are worth more than that! Just ask God.*

# *Warning!*

## *Fashion Magazines Can Be Dangerous to Your Health*

*by Vicki Courtney*

By now you have probably been warned about the dangers of smoking. You have probably been warned about the dangers of drinking and drugs. But have you ever been warned about the dangers of fashion magazines? I get it. Sometimes it's fun to pick up an actual hard copy of a teen or women's magazine and thumb through the pages in your down time. Maybe you're in a waiting room and lured by a subtitle that promises a new, improved, sexy you. Seems pretty harmless, right? Wrong. One study found that women were negatively affected after viewing pictures of models in magazine ads for just three minutes.[1]

What really gets me is that fashion magazines (both print and online) will feature damage-control articles or posts that encourage women to accept and embrace their body shapes. Yet if you glance through the images, you would be hard-pressed to find a model that represents the average American woman, who is a size twelve or fourteen. Ditto for the online fashion blogs. Whether online or in print, their encouragement to "be happy with who you are" rings hollow when you take a closer look at the models they choose. I believe there is a word that describes that kind of behavior—hypocrisy.

But that's not the only way fashion magazines demonstrate hypocrisy. They preach "girl power" and encourage girls to be independent and strong, yet the articles are often filled with advice about what it takes to get a guy's attention. They tell you what to wear to make guys drool, or what to do to keep a guy—resulting in the overall message that you are a big nothing unless you have a guy on your arm. Sure, girls are going to like guys, but wouldn't it be better if we attracted them with our minds and hearts rather than "snag-a-man" tactics? Girls and women are portrayed as sex objects, and the message is that we are here in this world to please and satisfy men. Some girl power, huh? I assure you, you are worth more than that.

And what about the endorsement of sexual activity? I could fill an entire book with blatant examples of ways magazine articles, advertisements, and advice columns imply that sex is nothing more than a recreational hobby. They make it seem like everyone is doing it, and you're some kind of freak if you're still a virgin. Many of the writers and editors of these magazines defend their content by saying this is what girls really want to hear. That's a cop-out. The bottom line is, in order to attract consumers and make money, the magazines have to push the limit with their content. Don't be fooled—they are not looking out for you. In fact, they are using you to make money. They are laughing all the way to the bank while teen girls flip through their pages and scroll through their sites, becoming more and more disillusioned and depressed with every minute that goes by.

Why pay for a product that leaves a majority of girls feeling depressed? Or for that matter, why waste a single valuable minute of your day if you end up feeling disillusioned? If you care at all about your emotional well-being, stay far away from fashion magazines and choose your online resources carefully. Don't let photoshopped celebrity images and negative articles cause you to question your worth. Instead, search the pages of Scripture and discover who you are from the source that never changes.

***Source:***

1. "Women Of All Sizes Feel Badly About Their Bodies After Seeing Models"; March 27, 2007; University of Missouri-Columbia. https://www.sciencedaily.com/releases/2007/03/070326152704.htm.

# WISE WORDS FROM COLLEGE GIRLS

*by Ashley Anderson*

We asked a group of college girls to share their thoughts on struggles they faced at your age and what they've learned in the years since. Here's what they had to say about body image and the pressure to conform . . .

## *Lezli, 21*

Every woman's body is different. I can get caught up in the numbers on a scale until I realize that they mean nothing—I feel best when I am eating a balanced diet and exercising because keeping my body healthy is glorifying God.

## *Charli, 20*

Growing up, I was always self-conscious about my weight and being bigger than everyone else, but I had already tried every diet without success. I eventually learned to feel okay in my own skin. I was happier once I stopped letting others dictate how I felt about myself and started living for God.

## *Jenna, 22*

I don't know about you, but I think that if the one who made all the stars in the sky also made me, then He must have known what He was doing. God makes no mistakes. He has made everyone different according to how He saw it was meant to be. Embrace who you are, how you have been created, and lean on the truth that you were wonderfully and fearfully made.

## *Janie, 20*

You are not alone in your hateful thoughts about your body. I have struggled with self-image for as long as I can remember. It's hard for me to walk by a mirror and not entertain a negative thought about my appearance. I have found the most freedom from the exhausting obsession over my looks through *surrender*. Waking up every day and saying, "Jesus, this day is Yours. My life is Yours. Transform my mind and transform the way I see myself today."

### Katie, 20

What I've found true is that the more I fall in love with the Lord, the more I recognize His truths for me, including that He made me *perfect* and beautiful and unique. The more time I spend with Him, the less I struggle with how I outwardly look because I know He wants nothing but my heart.

### Caitlin, 22

While on the competitive dance team in college, I was constantly surrounded by women who counted their calories and looked to eating disorders as a normal way of keep their weight down. To go about losing weight the wrong way—with a selfish desire, not with a healthy lifestyle—is comparable to insulting God's work of art. As a child of God, you will always be beautiful inside and out, regardless of what the scale may say.

### Kaitlyn, 22

All girls struggle with comparison, so luckily you are not alone! I've always had super pale skin (basically baby powder white), and I was very insecure about this because everyone around me was so cute and tan. Finally I realized that everyone has things they are insecure about, but God made us how we are for a reason, and He calls us beautiful.

### Caroline, 21

When I was in eighth grade, a girl asked me if I ever tried to cover up my freckles with makeup. I had never really thought anything of my freckles—everyone in my family had them as well—but her comment made me realize that none of the "cool" girls in my grade had freckles, fair skin, and curly hair. As I grew in my faith, I realized that these qualities were what made me unique, and decided I would try to love them. My camp counselor told me that God didn't mess up on anything, so what makes me think He messed up on me? Find the thing that makes you unique and think about God crafting that very quality, excited and proud of His creation.

### Carly, 22

I think the hardest part of thinking about body image is our unrealistic expectations of ourselves. How on earth could we all weigh 115 pounds and wear a size zero? How boring and so unlike Christ for Him to make us all the same. Be beautiful in your own skin because you display a piece of God that no one else can.

### Claire, 22

As girls, we look at our own bodies through highly critical eyes. We see flaws in our bodies that other people would never even begin to notice. The one thing you hate about your body, whether it be your skin tone, nose, long legs, short legs, whatever that one trait is, there's another girl out there who would disagree and actually envy that trait. Encourage others as you embrace your own beauty.

### Hannah, 22

One thing I know is true is that I will never catch up to or be satisfied by the standard of the world. Yet God calls us not to worry about what we eat or what we wear. He calls us daughters, and He has made us perfect through believing in the death of His Son. He is truth, and His standard is the only one that will not waver.

### Alyssa, 21

I struggled deeply, and still often do, with comparison. The biggest way this hit me in middle school and high school was through body image. I was insecure about how my body differed from other girls and had a continuous fear that I would only be more dissatisfied as I aged. But the more I spent time with Jesus, the more I was reminded that the God who made everything said that He made me perfectly and that He delighted in me. Some days I believe this more than others, but it is a truth that I can repeat to myself with confidence.

### Bailey, 22

The perfect Creator made *you* specifically. Don't insult Him by wishing you were different.

### Emma, 22

Battling an eating disorder was the most miserable thing I've ever experienced. I wanted control over my body, but I was giving that control to other people when I put so much value in their judgment. It took me a very long time to fully comprehend the importance of what it means to be a child of God—my body and I belong to God, as does my self-worth and my self-esteem. Follow Him on the path to righteousness. Your body is a temple, and more importantly, it isn't yours to begin with. It's God's. It's a gift. Treat it as such.

# Are You the Eating Disorder Type?

*by Vicki Courtney*

On a recent trip to Starbucks, the woman in front of me ordered a low-fat-grande-vanilla-no-foam-two-Sweet'N-Lows-decaf-latte. In the time it took her to say it, I could have taken a short vacation. Clearly, this gal was on a diet. I recognized the familiar diet language from my own past experience of trying to shave every calorie off a latte yet still have something left in the cup. Ah, the fond memories of a chronic dieter. As I stepped up to the counter, I felt a twinge of guilt as I ordered a vanilla latte with all the extras. Give me the foam, the sugar, the whole milk. Was I experiencing a weak moment of abandoned willpower? Not exactly. You see, I used to have an eating disorder. Fortunately, my disorder never required hospitalization, but a few times my weight plunged as low as one hundred pounds on my five-foot, five-inch frame. I now consider myself recovered, but I still wrestle from time to time with the temptation to "control" my weight by limiting necessary calories.

My love/hate relationship with food began in college. During my freshman year, I gained the traditional "freshman 10," and a few pounds to boot. Prior to that time, I had always been the athletic type and on the thin side. Weight had never been a problem for me until college. Dorm food, fast food, and food at all hours of the day and night without exercise began to take its toll. During college, my weight fluctuated by as much as thirty pounds. At one point I was just a few pounds over the double digits. I was living on saltines, fruit, and diet sodas, and was obsessed with working out, sometimes twice a day. My wake-up call came when I passed out at the health club during a workout. Any resolve I made to "get better" was short-lived, and before long food was once again my enemy. This attitude consumed my thinking each and every day of my college years. If my weight topped 110 pounds, I felt guilty, miserable, and disgusted with myself.

It is estimated that as many as one-third of high-school girls show some symptoms of an eating disorder.[1] Even if you don't have an eating disorder, chances are, you know someone who does. I am not a professional counselor, but I want to offer you some basic truths that helped me in my own recovery.

There are three basic aspects of eating disorders:

***1. The physical aspect.*** The body responds to starvation by slowing certain bodily processes. Other possible side effects are a decrease in blood pressure, slowed breathing, and an end to menstruation. Skin can become dry, and hair and nails become brittle. Reduced fat causes the body temperature to fall. As body chemicals become imbalanced, heart failure can occur.[2]

***2. The emotional aspect.*** I remember when my concerned parents would tell me, "Just eat!" Though their motives were pure, it is similar to telling an alcoholic, "Just stop drinking!" When attempting to help someone with an eating disorder, one cannot beg them to eat or give them facts about the damage they are doing to their body. Beneath the surface of every eating disorder is a feeling of low self-worth and disgust in regard to body image. For some it will stem from a control issue. When other things in life are in disarray, there is a sense of comfort in being able to control at least one area of your life—your weight. My three most serious bouts with anorexia came at times when I perceived circumstances in my life as out of my control.

For others, it will serve as a way to get attention. Unfortunately, many people will unknowingly encourage the sufferer by paying compliments to someone with a borderline eating disorder. I was amazed at the amount of favorable praise I received from girls in high school and college when I had an eating disorder. I looked like a frail skeleton, yet girls would say, "You look great!" My all-time favorite was, "What is your secret to staying so thin?" Amazingly, the comments that most infuriated me came from only a handful of friends. They had the boldness to be honest about the situation and say, "You look terrible," or, "Are you okay? I'm worried about you." Their negative form of attention, though unwelcome at the time, eventually motivated me in my quest to get better.

***3. The spiritual aspect.*** When someone is deep in the throes of an eating disorder, building a relationship with Jesus Christ is rarely at the top of their priority list. They are consumed with food—not Christ. In John 5:6, Jesus asked a disabled man by the pool of Bethesda before He healed him, "Do you want to get well?" It seems strange that Jesus would ask this of someone who had been lame for thirty-eight years, yet it is a critical question in a healing process.

If you have an eating disorder, can you take the first step by answering the question Jesus posed to the disabled man? Do you want to get well? If your answer is a confident yes, then share with someone you trust that you need help. My first step in the healing process came when I was finally able to acknowledge, "I want to get well." Acknowledging that you have a problem is only the first step, and it may be necessary to see a Christian counselor or someone in the medical field if your condition is serious. If you are ready, help is on the way. The Great Physician is in . . . will you see Him?

***Sources:***

1. "Eating Disorders in Teens," *Dr. Greene*, last modified March 29, 2001, http://www.drgreene.com/eating-disorders-teens.

2. Dixie Farley, "On the Teen Scene: Eating Disorders Required Medical Attention," *Kid Source Online*, http://www.kidsource.com/kidsource/content4/eating.disorder.fda.html.

# EXERCISE: THE NEW OBSESSION

*by Pam Gibbs*

If a little exercise is good for your body, then exercising *a lot* should be even better, right?

Not necessarily.

Sometimes exercising can lead to physical injuries—and more.

Scientists call it exercise obsession. You probably won't hear anybody else use those words. Think of it as exercising too much and too often.

So what is it, exactly?

Being obsessed with exercise will look different for every person, but most girls who struggle with it show some common signs. See if any of these describe you:

1. You feel restless and cranky when you skip exercising a day or two.
2. Your friends and family worry that you work out too much.
3. You try to cut back on the exercise, but you just can't stand it.
4. You spend all of your free time exercising or thinking about it.
5. You won't allow yourself to eat anything unhealthy (such as cupcakes or ice cream) without exercising to burn off the calories.
6. You practice sports at school, then spend another hour working out when you get home.
7. You keep working out (running, lifting weights, going to a class) even though you are hurt and your body needs to heal.
8. You define your self-worth by the way your body looks (or how much you work out).
9. You give up time with friends so you can work out more.

So what's the big deal? Why not exercise a lot? After all, everyone from Michelle Obama to your gym teacher is telling you to get more exercise. Here are a few good reasons you might want to be careful about your workout habits:

1. Your hormones will get out of whack. When that happens, it can change your menstrual cycle (when you get your period), or stop your cycle altogether.

The upheaval can also increase your risk of bone loss. I know you aren't worried about this now, but you will later. Trust me—you don't want to mess up the delicate balance of hormones in your body.

2. Excessive exercise can weaken your body. You can damage bones, cartilage, tendons, joints, and ligaments. And instead of building muscle, you could be destroying muscles, especially if you're not eating right. Without the right nutrients, your body will break down muscle for energy. Not good.

3. Other parts of your life suffer. When exercising becomes the priority, other things bear the consequences—such as your friends and family members. Or your schoolwork. Or your relationship with God. Yikes!

4. You could get depressed. Believe it or not, exercising can cause your emotions to take a downturn. Girls begin to think that they are only worthy of love and acceptance when they are fit and trim. They begin to believe the lies of culture that say a popular girl can only wear a size two. Seriously. My dog can't fit into some of the shirts displayed on the sales floor of teen clothing hot spots.

Does this mean you shouldn't exercise? No. Is it okay to take a study break by going for a run? Absolutely. The key is balance. Anytime one aspect of your life becomes all-consuming, you're in trouble—whether that's a boyfriend, a hobby, or exercising. God wants you to take care of His temple. But you can abuse it by working out too much. It's okay to take a few days off. Your friends, family, and body will be glad you did.

## How do you know you need a break?

1. You have zero motivation. If you're dreading that run (more than normal!), you might need a day off.

2. You can't sleep. Normally, a bike ride during the day would help you sleep better in the evening. However, if you exercise too much, you raise the levels of cortisol in your body, which keeps you from being able to sleep.

3. Your heart rate is too high. Obviously, your heart will race after you run, but if you wake up in the morning to find that your heart rate is higher than it should be, that's an indication to take a break for a couple of days.

4. You feel sluggish. For most people, working out alleviates that tired and sluggish feeling. But if you have spent too much time at the gym, the exercise will only exhaust your body. The leaner and stronger you become, the more time your body will need to recover.

# EXTREME MAKEOVER

*by Vicki Courtney*

My daughter was one of those beautiful babies who got attention everywhere she went. She was extremely small for her age and had beautiful fair skin, blonde curly hair, blue eyes, and a sparkling personality. When she started walking, people often oohed and aahed and commented that she looked like a walking porcelain china doll. In the beginning, I loved the attention she got and would smile proudly when people complimented her.

I remember one time when she was about three years old, she said something to indicate that she was well aware of the attention she got for her looks. We were walking along a sidewalk, and she caught a glimpse of her reflection in a shop window and said, "Ooh, pwiddy gull." At the time I thought it was perfectly adorable, and it indicated her high self-esteem. Unfortunately, I was still buying into the world's worth equation: that worth equals what you look like. By default, I had pushed the same faulty equation off on my daughter.

However, about a year later when she was in preschool, I realized we had a problem. It was picture day at her school, and she put on her prettiest dress with the matching hair ribbon. When I dropped her off at the door that morning, her teacher said, "Paige, you are such a pretty girl." And instead of saying thank you, my child brushed by her teacher with a sideways glance and said, "I know. Everyone tells me that." I was mortified!

After that, I quit making comments about her outer beauty and tried to downplay it when others complimented her. Besides, everyone knows that cute kids don't always grow up to be cute adults. If I had continued to allow her to define her worth by her outward appearance, I would be setting her up for a world of hurt when she hit the gawky preteen years. Fortunately, today, as a young adult, she is not the least bit haughty or proud. She does not build her worth on anything as hollow as fading beauty.

This longing to feel beautiful permeates our culture. I recall a reality show that aired in 2004 called *The Swan* that took plain-looking women and offered to turn them into beautiful swans with extensive plastic surgery. I cringed when I heard contestants talk about how their "self-worth" was improved after having multiple surgical procedures. I wondered at the time what would happen when the natural aging process kicked into effect and things started to fall apart. Or what would happen if the women gained the weight back? Or what would happen if people stopped complimenting their appearance? I wondered if the contestants would still feel beautiful ten or fifteen years later.

Well, the verdict is in. One contestant, Lorrie Arias, who had $300,000 worth of plastic surgery, was interviewed a decade later. She said she is depressed, bipolar, agoraphobic, and suffers from body dysmorphic disorder. She has regained the weight and refuses to leave her home, except to see her therapist every few months. "I thought a tummy tuck would give me all the self-esteem in the world. Of course, it didn't. All I want now is for my story to help others, so they won't think that going under the knife is a cure-all," she said. "For a while it may be, but everything still comes back up."[1]

Beauty is not defined by physical appearance. If you base your worth on how you look on the outside, your self-esteem will be at the mercy of your mirror, your scale, and the opinions of others. True worth is only found by seeing yourself through God's eyes. God is in the business of makeovers, and He begins with your heart. No matter what you look like, you are beautiful to God.

*True worth is only found by seeing yourself through God's eyes.*

**Source:**

1. Laura Duca, "What It's Really Like to Get Extreme Plastic Surgery, from a Former 'Swan' Contestant," *Huffington Post*, last modified October 27, 2014, http://www.huffingtonpost.com/2014/10/27/extreme-plastic-surgery_n_6036110.html.

# QUICK *BEAUTY TIPS*

*by Vicki Courtney*

You've probably heard your mom say that "beauty comes from the inside" and thought, *Yeah, right, Mom—tell the guys that.* Well, believe it or not, your mom is right. So, what really makes a girl attractive? Try these beauty secrets:

## SMILE

If you haven't discovered this "free face-lift," try smiling more often. It will brighten your entire face.

## EYE CONTACT

Make direct eye contact when you are speaking with someone. When you nervously avert your eyes, it makes you look insecure.

## VOICE

Does your voice sound confident and mature? Some girls carry their "baby talk" voice into their adult years, and it is not attractive. Believe it or not, the maturity of your voice and your ability to carry on a conversation will be of critical importance when it comes time for you to find a job.

## POSTURE

When I was your age, my mother used to constantly tell me to quit slumping my shoulders and to stand up straight. It drove me crazy . . . until I saw a picture of myself and was horrified! My posture made me look so insecure that I made a concentrated effort to pull my shoulders back and stand taller.

## COMPASSION

If someone is hurting, do you make an effort to speak comforting words to them? A simple "I'm sorry you're going through that. Is there anything I can do to help?" goes a long way. Most importantly, it reveals the beauty in your heart.

## OUTWARD FOCUS

If a friend shares a difficulty with you or expresses sadness over something, do you remember to ask them how they are doing the next time you see them? It may even merit a phone call or text to check on them.

## SERVANT'S HEART

I am shocked at the number of people who have never been taught to look out for the needy. I have watched teenagers brush past elderly people, practically knocking them over when heading through a door. If you see someone in need, elderly or not, offer to help them. A servant's heart is one of the most beautiful character qualities there is.

## TREATING YOUR FAMILY WELL

There is nothing more unattractive than a girl snapping sarcastically at her parents or her siblings in public. If this is a problem for you, learn to hold your tongue and express yourself when the time is right.

## HUMOR

Have you learned to laugh at yourself when you do something embarrassing? Everyone blows it from time to time, whether they trip and fall or say something totally idiotic. Rather than be mortified, crack up! If you don't make a big deal of it, chances are, no one else will either.

## ADMITTING WEAKNESSES AND FLAWS

Everyone has weaknesses—it's a fact. Can you admit to yours when they show up, or do you pretend as though you always have your act together?

## REJOICING WITH OTHERS

Very few people (including Christians) can sincerely be happy when others around them succeed. However, those who rejoice when others rejoice display their beauty for all to see.

## ATTITUDE

Have you noticed how your attitude can affect an outcome? You can't always change your circumstances, but you can choose your attitude.

## CONFIDENCE

There is a big difference between being confident and being conceited. Confidence comes from being sure of yourself because you appreciate the gifts God has given you. Conceit is when you have a high opinion of yourself and take the credit for your giftedness.

## BEING YOURSELF

Most teens will knock themselves out trying to conform to the culture around them. Rare is the girl who is truly authentic and comfortable with herself. Don't be a pretender. You are a unique creation of God.

## FAITH

A girl who loves Jesus more than life can't help but shine from the inside out. She will brighten every room she enters, and her glow for Christ will be contagious.

# Is It Okay to Feel Beautiful?

*by Ali Claxton*

As Christians, we talk so much about inward beauty that it may seem like our outward appearance is something to be downplayed. Is it okay to celebrate physical beauty? Can we enjoy dressing cute and spending time on hair and makeup in a way that honors God? I think the answer is yes, if we have an accurate view of beauty.

Beauty has been a defining aspect of humanity since the very beginning. God has given each person unique features and intricate details to reflect His glory. Psalm 139 describes the purposeful and beautiful way God designed us—not just spiritually, but physically. His creative nature is on display through our physical bodies, and for that reason alone, we should celebrate beauty.

When our identity is rooted in God's truth, we see ourselves differently. When we consider how His hands created us, we can praise God for the fact that we are "fearfully and wonderfully made" (Psalm 139:14 NIV). We shouldn't nitpick every flaw or obsess over things we want to change about our appearance. We don't need to compare ourselves to every magazine cover or even to images of friends on social media. We can live with the contentment of knowing that beauty begins on the inside and works its way out. Even amid a culture that elevates physical appearance above all else, we can believe God's definition of beauty.

A woman who is beautiful by appearance alone will not stay that way in the eyes of those she interacts with. If she is full of pride and obsessed with her looks, it doesn't take long for her beauty to fade. The opposite is also true. A girl whom society might deem as "ordinary" or nondescript can light up a room with a smile, and radiance can stem from her inner confidence. That's how we can celebrate beauty: we carry ourselves in such a way that people are drawn to *who* we are rather than to what we look like.

We find stories in Scripture that point to this reality. Take Esther, for example. Esther's physical beauty placed her in a unique position to bring God glory. What if Esther had refused to see herself as beautiful enough to make an appeal to her husband, the king? Had she ignored the opportunity that her appearance presented, she would have missed out on God's incredible plan for her life. On the other hand, what if Esther had obsessed over her physical beauty? Had she simply sat on her throne looking glamorous, countless people would have perished in the wake of her arrogance, including herself. Thankfully, that's not what happened. Esther's physical beauty was part of her story, but it wasn't her greatest quality. She trusted God's sovereignty and let Him use every aspect of her life for His purposes—including her outward appearance.

Celebrating the beauty God has innately given us is an act of worship when our gaze is set on Him and not ourselves. We don't have to "let ourselves go" in order to live godly lives. In fact, we are called to honor God with our bodies, not abuse or neglect them. We can and should enjoy dressing up, fixing our hair, and feeling confident in how we present ourselves to the world. But keep this in mind: the true test of beauty is the motive behind what we do. When appearance becomes a measure of worth or a means of drawing attention to ourselves, we've lost sight of what really matters. True beauty is always a reflection of our Creator and a cause to celebrate Him! Our inner beauty and outer beauty are inseparable in His eyes because they are part of the same wonderful design. Let your confidence rest in that reality.

## TEN TRAITS THAT DIMINISH YOUR BEAUTY

1. Arrogance

2. Envy

3. Self-centeredness

4. Anger

5. Materialism

6. Self-pity

7. Cynicism

8. Vanity

9. Greed

10. Meanness

# Think This, Not That

*by Tami Overhauser*

One of the first things you do in the morning is look in the mirror. Why not start the day by getting your thoughts rolling in the right direction? Replace any negative thoughts with God's empowering Word and see if your image starts to "reflect" your new positive confessions!

Philippians 4:8 encourages us to fix our eyes on what is true and good; to spend our time thinking about things that are pure and lovely; to dwell on things that are excellent and worthy of praise. Look up the following verses this week. Think about the truths they represent every time you glance in the mirror:

*You are fearfully and wonderfully made.*
*—Psalm 139:14*

*You are made up of more than just your outward appearance.—1 Samuel 16:7*

*You are loved with an everlasting love.*
*—Jeremiah 31:3*

*You are the work of God's hand.—Isaiah 64:8*

*You are chosen and handpicked by God.*
*—2 Thessalonians 2:13*

You are beautiful and prosperous, like a royal crown in His hand.—Isaiah 62:3

You are beautiful.—Ecclesiastes 3:11

You are His child.—John 1:12

You are dearly loved.—Colossians 3:12

You are infinitely valuable to Him.—Luke 12:7

You are God's treasured possession.—1 Peter 2:9

You are forgiven.—Hebrews 8:12

You are being transformed into His likeness.
—2 Corinthians 3:18

You are cared for.—Luke 12:22–24

You are beautiful from the inside out.—1 Peter 3:3–4

# That Thing You Do

# When I Grow Up

*by Vicki Courtney*

Have you ever known people who have the next twenty years of life already planned out? They seem to know exactly what career path to take, when (or if) they want to get married, how many kids they will have, where they want to live, and what sort of house they will live in. Some of them have it down to the color of paint on the walls. I call it living by a checklist.

I'm not much into checklists, but at your age, I was fairly certain that I had it all figured out, at least when it came to a career. I wanted to be a lawyer. In fact, when I got to college, I declared myself a pre-law major. That lasted all of about one semester before I changed my major to business, then communications, then sociology, then economics. Okay, so maybe I didn't have everything figured out after all.

After five years in college and changing my major five times, I finally graduated with a degree in economics. A career counselor told me that most people with degrees in economics pursue jobs in the banking industry. Hmm . . . I had spent a lot of time in banks in my college years, but it was usually to sort out overdrafts on my checking account. Probably not a good field for me, considering I couldn't even balance my own checkbook. Fast-forward thirty years, and I still can't balance a checkbook. Thank goodness I didn't go to work in a bank because I might not have figured out that I was supposed to be a writer all along.

## MY UNREAL LIST

1. Be Homecoming Queen.
2. Go to college at Duke.
3. Meet Mr. Right.
4. Get into law school.
5. Become a lawyer.
6. Have first child (boy).
7. Make partner in the law firm.
8. Have second child (girl).
9. Retire at age fifty-five.
10. Live happily ever after.

And do you know how I figured out that I was supposed to be a writer? After I was married and had my first child, I began sending out Christmas letters every year to my friends and family. I always hated getting Christmas letters from people who had perfect kids and perfect lives. You know, the ones where "Little Johnny just turned one and can sing his ABCs in English, Spanish, and French, blindfolded while tap dancing." The next year the letter informs us he's getting recruitment letters from the ivy-league colleges. They may as well just skip all the bragging and get to the real reason they are sending the letter—it's their sophisticated way of saying, "We're better than you! Our family is cooler, better looking, and more successful than yours." So, when I wrote my letter each year, I decided to be honest. One time I even wrote about how my happy, little cherubs had duked it out and called each other "dummy poop heads" while posing for the Christmas picture that went along with the letter. Another time I wrote about my daughter's habit of disrobing in public. Don't worry—she was a toddler at the time.

I was candidly honest, and a funny thing happened. Every year when I sent out the letter, people would tell me how they looked forward to my letter because they knew it would make them laugh. Over and over again they would tell me, "You know, you should think about writing." I didn't take a single writing class in college, and I had never once considered being a writer when I was your age. And here I am today, a writer. Go figure.

A really good friend of mine said she knew what she wanted to be when she grew up from the time she was a little girl. She wanted to be a doctor. She graduated in the top of her class, went to college, was accepted into medical school, got married, and finally realized her dream of becoming a doctor. There was only one problem: When she started her practice, she'd just had her first child. As the days went on, it became harder and harder for her to leave her baby with the nanny so she could have her dream job. She stuck with her "checklist" but was torn.

One day when she came home, the nanny told her not to fix any more bottles for the baby. The nanny had weaned the baby from the bottle and taught him to drink from a cup. That was really tough on my friend because she wanted to be the one to experience her baby's milestones. The straw that broke the camel's back came a couple months later when the nanny informed her the baby had taken his first steps and my friend had missed it. She told me it was at that point she realized no matter how careful she had been to plan the details of her future, she hadn't factored in how she might feel as a mother when pursuing her lifelong dream job. Today she still practices medicine, but only part-time. She has other important matters to tend to, like soccer games and trips to the park. She also had two more kids and made sure she was around to see their milestones.

My point is this: it's impossible to plan for the future and factor in all the details when you don't know those details yet. Resist the urge to draw a road map for your life. If you live your life by a checklist, it allows God little room to direct your steps. There is nothing wrong with having an idea of what you might like your future to be, but don't go overboard by micromanaging every aspect. Besides, God may not see eye-to-eye with everything on your checklist. Or, as my friend learned, He may add something to the list that is far better than that dream job. Leave room for God to move. There is plenty of time for Him to reveal His plan and purpose for your life. In the meantime, sit back and enjoy the ride.

We can make our plans, but the LORD determines our steps.
—Proverbs 16:9 NLT

# WHAT WERE YOU CREATED TO DO?

*by Ali Claxton*

Amid a culture that values great achievements, people go to extraordinary lengths to pursue goals and become known for their accomplishments. From childhood, we are challenged to do more, try harder, reach higher. We compare our talents to others' talents and compete for opportunities. We even label ourselves by what we do. In certain situations, we introduce ourselves with a description of what we're good at: "Hi, my name is _____, and I'm a _____ (cheerleader, dancer, musician, honor student, etc.)." This habit doesn't go away in adulthood. It actually becomes second nature to describe who we are based on what we do for a living.

How much of our existence is wrapped up in what we do? Is our worth measured by how much we accomplish? For those who believe that, life becomes an endless pursuit. People work diligently, day in and day out, but they never do quite enough to feel validated. Contentment remains just beyond reach.

That's not how God intended for us to live. The biblical perspective of worth tells us that we are valuable because of who we are, not what we do. God's grace isn't contingent upon what we accomplish in this life. We can't earn God's affection or get His attention with lofty goals and great achievements. It doesn't work that way. He is infinitely more concerned with who we are than what we do. That's because what we do is actually a reflection of who we are, not the other way around.

Understanding that our worth isn't measured by what we accomplish should instill in us a sense of peace and belonging. But this assurance isn't an excuse to sit back and waste our days here on earth. Following Jesus never leads to apathy and laziness. God has a purpose and plan for each of our lives; He has uniquely gifted us, and we are called to steward well the talents and opportunities He has entrusted to us. What we do with the life God gives us matters.

We were created to glorify God. Though our primary purpose is the same, how we go about glorifying God with our lives will look different for each of us. That's because God designed us with unique qualities and passions. Doing what you were created to do isn't merely about excelling in sports, making straight As, or pursuing your dream career. It's about using your time, talents, resources, and opportunities to honor God and reflect His glory in this world. Every aspect of your life—everything you do and say—reflects who you are and Who you belong to. So whether you become a doctor, lawyer, social worker, teacher, musician, missionary, accountant, or stay-at-home mom (or whatever else), you are called to do that work in His name and for His glory.

You don't have to spend your life worrying about whether you are in the perfect job or doing ministry in the one place on earth God wants to use you. His dreams for you aren't tied to positions or titles or geographic locations. Yes, there are jobs and opportunities that will more naturally fit your skills and passions, but God isn't running a cosmic corporation. He is accomplishing kingdom work in this world, and you've been invited to join in. You have opportunities every day to do things that honor Him and reflect His character. Don't waste a moment. Start doing what you were created to do.

For we are His creation, created in Christ Jesus for good works, which God prepared ahead of time so that we should walk in them. —Ephesians 2:10

I am sure of this, that He who started a good work in you will carry it on to completion until the day of Christ Jesus. —Philippians 1:6

LORD my God, You have done many things—Your wonderful works and Your plans for us; none can compare with You. If I were to report and speak of them, they are more than can be told. —Psalm 40:5

Now to Him who is able to do above and beyond all that we ask or think according to the power that works in us—to Him be glory in the church and in Christ Jesus. —Ephesians 3:20–21

Whatever you do, do it enthusiastically, as something done for the Lord and not for men, knowing that you will receive the reward of an inheritance from the Lord. You serve the Lord Christ. —Colossians 3:23–24

# Dare To Be Brave

*by Tami Overhauser*

### What would you attempt to do if you knew you couldn't fail?

**Olivia, 14**
I would dance.

**Grace, 13**
I would be an Olympic volleyball player or maybe an astronaut.

**Annabella, 14**
I would be an Olympic swimmer.

**Elisha, 15**
I would pursue acting.

**Georgia, 13**
I would tell everyone about Jesus.

**Kailey, 15**
I would preach around the world.

**Rebekah, 16**
I would travel the world and be a marine biologist or maybe even become the president.

**Samantha, 14**
I would be a famous artist with my work in famous galleries.

**Brittany, 15**
I would audition for Broadway.

### Emma, 17

I would start a successful non-profit.

### Anna, 14

I would sing and play the guitar.

### Amy Lynne, 17

I would be a singer.

### Becca, 15

I would love to have an amazing voice and sing lead vocals in church.

### Kyra, 15

I would end world hunger.

### Sophia, 16

I would start my own event-planning company.

### Isa, 17

I would compete in the X Games for snowboarding.

### Claire, 16

I would encourage people to be the best they can and to never give up.

### Sophia, 17

I would own a successful business.

### Tate, 14

I would love to be good at sports.

I can do all things through Christ who strengthens me.—Philippians 4:13 NKJV

Let your light shine before others.—Matthew 5:16 ESV

Delight yourself in the LORD, and he will give you the desires of your heart.—Psalm 37:4 ESV

The LORD directs the steps of the godly. He delights in every detail of their lives.—Psalm 37:23 NLT

The heart of man plans his way, but the LORD establishes his steps.—Proverbs 16:9 ESV

Commit your way to the LORD; trust in him, and he will act.—Psalm 37:5 ESV

Be strong and courageous.—Joshua 1:9 ESV

The righteous are bold as a lion.—Proverbs 28:1 ESV

# Quiz: Get Real!

Everyone hates a fake—so start getting honest with yourself and God! Take this quiz and find out if the real you needs a spiritual makeover. What would you do in each of the following scenarios?

1. **It's the end of the day, and you haven't made time for God. You . . .**
   A. say a quick good-night prayer and hit the sheets.
   B. make some quality time with God before you snooze.
   C. don't really think about it and text your friends before catching some z's.

2. **Your science teacher openly ridicules Christians in class. You . . .**
   A. stay silent, hoping he won't remember you are a Christian.
   B. stand up for what is right, even though your grades might take a beating.
   C. join in, even though that's not how you really feel inside.

3. **Your best friend wants you to skip last period with her and go to the lake. You . . .**
   A. tell her you aren't feeling well but would go if you felt better.
   B. decline and let her know dishonesty is a sin in your book. But you say you'll go to the lake another time when you don't have to skip school.
   C. give her the keys to your car and tell her to meet you in five minutes. (You have to change into your swimsuit first.)

4. **It's Friday night, and several close friends are going downtown with fake IDs to try to get into a popular club. You . . .**
   A. pretend you're grounded and tell them to be careful.
   B. remind them that you can't hang out with them if they're going to do illegal things. You encourage them to do something else instead.
   C. borrow your sister's old ID and tell your mom you're going to a girls' sleepover.

5. **You're sitting at youth group and the most unpopular girl sits down in the chair next to you. You . . .**
   A. stay where you are but convince your friends to come sit with you so you don't have to sit next to her by yourself.
   B. ask her how her week was, try to get to know her a little better, and invite her to dinner after youth group.
   C. pretend you have a phone call and go to the back to see where the cute guys are sitting.

6. **It's Monday morning, first period, and you forgot to do your math homework because you went out of town with your family. You . . .**
A. embellish the truth and ask for an extension.
B. tell your teacher you completely forgot and ask if you can turn it in tomorrow morning.
C. borrow your friend's homework and copy it quickly before class.

7. **You're at a friend's birthday party, and someone pulls out a bottle of alcohol. You . . .**
A. tell them you don't like the taste of alcohol but you'll stick around anyway.
B. let them know that underage drinking is wrong and politely excuse yourself to head home.
C. join in the fun and be the life of the party!

*If you answered mostly A:* Get a backbone. You know what's right but sometimes have a hard time standing up for what you believe. Find a Christian friend who can keep you accountable as well as encourage you to stand up for God. Get your approval from God and not your friends, and He will give you the courage to do what's right, even when everyone around you is making wrong choices.

*If you answered mostly B:* You get it—congratulations! You balance real life with godly values, and you're not afraid to stand up for what you believe. Your friends know you're not ashamed to be a Christian, and you stick to your Christian standards. Stay strong and continue to put God first in your life.

*If you answered mostly C:* Get a spiritual makeover. You crave the approval of your friends, which often leads to wrong choices or situations that leave you unsatisfied. Sin can be fun for a season, but eventually the separation from God leaves us feeling empty and alone. It's never too late to ask God to be the center of your life. Spend time with Him daily, and He will change your heart and desires. Eventually it won't matter what others are doing; you will realize you have a deeper peace when you obey God instead.

# GOOGLE-A-SINNER?

*by Vicki Courtney*

We've all made bad choices. We've done things we are embarrassed about or even ashamed of. What if those sins were made public for everyone to see? Believe it or not, some criminals have experienced a dose of public shame as part of the sentence for their crimes. Consider this:

In Maryland, Texas, Georgia, and California, shoplifters have been required to stand outside stores with signs announcing their crimes.

In Florida and Ohio, drunk drivers are issued special license plates that identify them to fellow motorists.

In Houston and Corpus Christi, Texas, convicted sex offenders have been ordered to place signs on their front lawns to inform families and children.

In Pennsylvania, a driver who caused a fatal accident was forced to carry a picture of the victim.

In North Carolina, four vandals who broke into a school and did sixty thousand dollars in damage were ordered to wear signs around their necks in public that read, "I Am a Juvenile Criminal."

One can only wonder if the public shame and humiliation deterred these criminals from committing future crimes. Aren't you glad that God doesn't keep a public ledger of our sins? Imagine for a minute what it would be like if you could simply Google someone's name, and up popped a chronological list of each and every sin that person had committed. Google-a-sinner at your fingertips. Date, time, nature of offense—all available for the public's viewing pleasure. And imagine how freaky it would be if it also listed the person's future sins. Think about how handy the list would be to potential employers, fiancées and fiancés, business partners, teachers, parents, or anyone looking for revealing information. Even if you'd want to Google other people's sin lists, you sure wouldn't want anyone to Google yours!

Let's take it a step further. Say that next to each sin, there is a rating from one to a hundred, depending on the severity of the offense. At the top, next to the person's name, is a number that represents the running total of every offense. You know how those fancy mattresses calculate a person's sleep number? Imagine if every person was given a "sin number." Even more humbling is the thought that each day, new sins are added to the list. In fact, just refreshing the page every hour might bring up pages of new sins—every thought, word, or deed that is not pleasing to God. Pretty scary, huh?

Fortunately, no one has access to our list of sins except for God. And for the Christian, the Bible is clear on what He does with the sins on that list. Psalm 103:12 says, "As far as the east is from the west, so far has He removed our transgressions from us." In case you are wondering how far it is between the east and the west, the two never meet. Holocaust survivor Corrie ten Boom once said that God casts our sins into the deepest ocean, then places a sign in the spot that says "No Fishing Allowed."

Unfortunately, a lot of people see God as some kind of angry judge. They imagine Him sitting behind a fancy mahogany desk with a gavel in hand, just waiting to lower the boom on anyone who misbehaves. Some Christians mistakenly believe that God is like some of the judges in the court cases mentioned above, forcing us to carry the burden and shame of our sins.

I'll admit, the whole concept of a loving God who forgives our sins is difficult to comprehend. When I became a Christian at the age of twenty-one, I had a hard time believing that God really forgave my sins and no longer held them against me. I mean, I had some real biggies on that sin list, and I figured He would want to punish me for them. I had already suffered the consequences of many of those sins, but it didn't seem like enough. I told people about His wonderful offer of forgiveness to those who believe in Jesus, but deep down, I wasn't sure I believed it for myself.

Certain sins on my sin list haunted me more than all the others. Even after becoming a Christian, I just couldn't believe that God would really forgive me for those sins. I beat myself up with so much shame that I'm surprised my knees didn't buckle from the weight of my guilt. And then one day, while attending a Christian women's event, the speaker shared a verse that I had heard a thousand times before. Something clicked, and God brought that verse to life in my heart. She was sharing about Jesus' death and reminded us of His final words on the cross. John 19:30 says, "When he had received the drink, Jesus said, 'It is finished.' With that, he bowed his head and gave up his spirit" (NIV).

Did you catch that? It is finished—a pretty simple statement that is loaded with life-changing meaning.

As I pondered the meaning and magnitude of that verse, it was as if God spoke these words to my heart: "Vicki, it is finished. The price has been paid. I didn't footnote My statement with any sort of conditions, such as, 'It is finished . . . unless you have had sex outside of marriage,' or, 'It is finished . . . unless you've had an abortion.' I just said, 'It is finished.' I no longer remember those sins. Child, it's time to lay them down." And lay them down, I did. I don't have the luxury of forgetting my sins, but when I remember them, I no longer feel shame. Instead, my shame has been replaced with an overflowing heart of gratitude for what God has done for me.

Hebrews 4:16 encourages us to "approach God's throne of grace with confidence, so that we may receive mercy and find grace to help us in our time of need" (NIV). Think of a time you needed grace—maybe you committed a sin so atrocious that you still feel uncomfortable at the thought of it. Now picture yourself approaching God's throne. You have an appointment with the King of kings and Lord of lords. He is waiting for you. You begin to approach the great Almighty. Do you walk? Do you run? Do you hang your head low and drag your feet? Once there, what do you say? Your answers to these questions will shed light on how you view God. Do you see Him as an angry judge who can't wait to punish you, or do you see Him as a loving Father who is ready and willing to forgive?

I am so grateful that I don't serve a God who would make me parade around town with a sign advertising my sins. I am glad that He does not make my sin list public for all to see. The truth is, every item on that list has been stamped with the word *forgiven*. What a comforting thought for Christians who have accepted His gift of forgiveness. If such a Google-a-sinner list did exist, anyone trying to access our mistakes would find this message instead: "Page no longer available. 'It is finished.' Love, God."

1. Do you see God as an angry judge or a loving Father?
2. Are you able to approach God's throne with grace and confidence over your sins?
3. If all sins are weighted equally in God's eyes, why do you think we are able to so easily dismiss the "little" sins in our lives? Is there really such a thing as a little sin?
4. Consider making a list of your sins on a piece of paper in private. When you are finished, read over it—and one at a time, scratch through each sin. Draw a cross over your paper, and at the top put, "It is finished."
5. God's forgiveness is often referred to as the "Good News." Why is that? Good news is always worth sharing, right?

# You Can Fail Without Being a Failure

*by Pam Gibbs*

## Complete this sentence: I am a _____.

You could have said a gazillion things . . .

> I am a girl.
>
> I am a cheerleader.
>
> I am a daughter, student, sister, driver.

Then you could have added some adjectives . . .

> I am a shy girl.
>
> I am a funny girl.
>
> I am a good cheerleader.
>
> I am a poor student.
>
> I am a great sister. (Yeah, I know, I'm stretching it a bit!)

Sometimes, though, you might define yourself in much different terms. For example, let's say you didn't make the cheer squad. Or you made a D on your latest English test. What if your science fair project bombed? Or you fell just before you crossed the finish line at a track meet? What then?

## I am a _____.

> What would you say about yourself?
>
> I am a failure.
>
> Is that what you said? Why?

Unfortunately, many of us would describe ourselves as failures. That's because we have bought into one of the biggest lies Satan will tell us: our worth equals how well we perform. Satan says that your worth is based on how well you do in sports. Or how funny you are. He will trick you into believing that your worth is based on your grades or your communication skills. Satan would have you believe that you are nothing more than your best success—or your worst failure. He will try to diminish those successes by reminding you of every embarrassing moment, bad grade, or angry word you've said.

# What Your Enemy Wants

Why would Satan want you to believe that lie? Because he doesn't want you to believe the truth about yourself. He wants you to forget that God has created you from scratch in His image (Genesis 1:27). He wants you to blow off scriptures that remind you of just how wonderfully and marvelously you've been made (Psalm 139:14). He doesn't want you to know that God created you "for good works, which God prepared ahead of time so that we should walk in them" (Ephesians 2:10). Satan wants you to live in defeat, terrified to risk the possibility of everyone else knowing you're a failure too.

If you adopt the huge lie that you're a failure, you'll stop trying to do anything significant. Senator Robert F. Kennedy once said, "Only those who dare to fail greatly can ever achieve greatly." If you're not willing to risk big in order to achieve big, then Satan has won. He doesn't have to worry about you doing anything big for God. Can you imagine what would happen if a generation of girls began to grasp their worth based on God's Word? If they embraced the truth of being made in God's image? If they sought God and asked Him to show them where He is at work so they could join Him?

What would you do if you weren't afraid of failure?

What would you do if you knew that the outcome wouldn't change your value, worth, or belonging?

Dream. For a minute, just think about what God might want you to do with your gifts and skills and passions and quirks. Then chase that dream. Whatever it is that you think God may have birthed in your heart to attempt to do for Him, with Him, and through His strength, go after it. Not to draw attention to yourself or show other people how awesome you are, but to put the spotlight on the One who created you and gifted you. Sing. Speak. Learn. Dance. Share. Jump. Run. Draw. Create. Give. Pray. Go. Try. And keep at it. Don't quit.

Live courageously. "Be strong and courageous. Do not be afraid; do not be discouraged, for the Lord your God will be with you wherever you go" (Joshua 1:9 niv). In the end, it doesn't matter whether you succeed or fail. What matters is giving glory to God in whatever you do (1 Corinthians 10:31). With that as your goal, you will never be a failure.

*Q.* *What would you do if you weren't afraid of failure?*

Scan for Video Answers!

# EPIC FAIL

*by Tami Overhauser*

*For though the righteous fall seven times,*
*they rise again.—Proverbs 24:16 NIV*

**H**ave you ever failed at something when you wanted badly to succeed? How did you feel? How did you respond to the setback? Maybe you cried or got frustrated or considered giving up. You may have even felt like your life was ruined. But don't give up just yet! You are not alone! Check out these dream chasers and world changers who failed at first but refused to see themselves as failures.

### Oprah Winfrey: *Talk Show Host and Media Mogul*
Oprah was fired from one of her first jobs because she was considered "unfit for TV."

### Vera Wang: *Fashion Designer*
Vera failed to make the US Olympic figure-skating team, then worked as an editor for *Vogue* and was denied a promotion. She eventually began designing wedding gowns at age forty, and today she is the top designer in the business.

### Meryl Streep: *Actress*
After failing to land a role, she nearly gave up on acting when a director caller her "too ugly." To date she has won three Academy Awards.

### Michael Jordan: *Basketball Player*
After being cut from his high school basketball team, a young Michael Jordan went home and cried alone in his bedroom. But Jordan didn't stop playing, and he didn't let this setback keep him back. He says, "I have failed over and over and over again in my life. And that is why I succeed."

### Babe Ruth: *Baseball Player*
Before holding his home run record, Babe held a pretty hefty strikeout record! When asked about this, he simply said, "Every strike brings me closer to the next home run."

### J. K. Rowling: *Novelist*

Before J. K. Rowling became successful, she was fired from a job because she would write stories on her work computer all day long. Luckily, that novel turned into the Harry Potter franchise, which has since made her a millionaire.

### Dr. Seuss: *Author*

Twenty-seven different publishers rejected his first book. He's now the most popular children's book author ever.

### Emily Dickinson: *Poet*

Though loved now, fewer than a dozen of her hundreds of poems were published during her lifetime.

### Walt Disney: *Entrepreneur*

Before Walt Disney built the empire we know today, a newspaper editor fired him because he "lacked imagination and had no good ideas."

### Vincent Van Gogh: *Painter*

While alive, he only sold one of his paintings to a friend for a small amount of money. He continued working throughout his life, and his paintings now are worth hundreds of millions of dollars.

### Albert Einstein: *Physicist*

We all know Einstein as a genius, but he wasn't known for his intelligence in his early years. He didn't speak until he was four years old and didn't read until he was seven. His teachers labeled him as mentally handicapped, but he later went on to win the Nobel Prize in physics!

### Thomas Edison: *Inventor*

Thomas Edison failed at least a thousand times before creating the light bulb.

### Steve Jobs: *Entrepreneur*

Steve Jobs was a college dropout and an unsuccessful businessman before he eventually created several iconic products, including the iPod, iPhone, and iPad. Jobs became one of the richest men in the world, and his inventions changed the face of technology forever.

### Bill Gates: *Business Investor and Inventor*

After he dropped out of Harvard, Gates started his first business, which flopped. Luckily, he tried again—and Microsoft was born.

### Abraham Lincoln: *Sixteenth US President*

Lincoln struggled in the military, failed at starting a business, and lost several runs for public office before becoming president.

### Steven Spielberg: *Director and Filmmaker*

Spielberg was rejected from the University of Southern California School of Cinematic Arts three times. After another school finally accepted him, he dropped out to pursue directing. His movies have won him dozens of awards, including three Oscars.

### Lady Gaga: *Singer and Songwriter*

When she was finally signed onto her first major record label, she was fired after only three months.

### Elvis Presley: *Singer*

After a performance at Nashville's Grand Ole Opry, the concert hall manager told Elvis that he was better off returning to Memphis and driving trucks—which had been his career.

### Harland David Sanders: *Businessman*

Over a thousand restaurants rejected Colonel Sanders's chicken, but today there are KFC restaurants bearing his image all over the world.[1]

Don't give up. Don't let one momentary failure define you. Let God teach you, develop you, and help you become everything He created you to be.

### *Source:*

1. Rachel Sugar, Richard Feloni, and Ashley Lutz, "29 Famous People Who Failed Before They Succeeded," *Business Insider*, last modified July 9, 2015, http://www.businessinsider.com/successful-people-who-failed-at-first-2015-7.

My grace is sufficient for you, for power is perfected in weakness. —2 Corinthians 12:9

My flesh and my heart may fail, but God is the strength of my heart and my portion forever. —Psalm 73:26 NASB

Now to Him who is able to do above and beyond all that we ask or think according to the power that works in us— to Him be glory . . . forever and ever. —Ephesians 3:20–21

Ask and it will be given to you; seek and you will find; knock and the door will be opened to you. —Matthew 7:7 NIV

For I know the plans I have for you, declares the LORD, plans for welfare and not for evil, to give you a future and a hope. —Jeremiah 29:11 ESV

# WISE WORDS FROM COLLEGE GIRLS

*by Ashley Anderson*

We asked a group of college girls to share their thoughts on struggles they faced at your age and what they've learned in the years since. Here's what they had to say about basing their worth on talents or achievements. . . .

## Jenna, 22

As girls growing up, we try to define ourselves by what we *do* instead of who we *are*—these two things are very different. We *will* make a bad grade, we *will* lose a game, we *will* lose some friends . . . and when this happens our whole identity crumbles around us. But if as girls we define ourselves by who we are—daughters of the one true King—then our identity is firm, set, and forever.

## Janie, 20

Colossians 3:13–14 says, "Bear with each other, and forgive each other. If someone does wrong to you, forgive that person because the Lord forgave you. Even more than all this, clothe yourself in love. Love is what holds you all together in perfect unity" (NCV). Wow, these verses are so against everything our culture teaches us. The world says, "Be on top. Win first place. Do whatever it takes to be the best. Second place is failing." Jesus says the opposite. He says take the backseat. Be okay with second place. Put others before you. Be selfless. We don't have to be in a competition against our friends, but rather unite with other girls to encourage and uplift one another and be on the same team!

## Mary Claire, 20

It has taken me twenty years to finally realize that I cannot do it on my own. I cannot do everything right. My hard work will not always pay off. *I will fail.* Over this past year, I have slowly started to open my tight grasp on my success. To experience freedom, you must give up control of your life. For me, it meant waking up every morning and physically opening my hands, which was one of the hardest parts for me, and saying, "I surrender." It also meant thinking about my day and letting go of my success. It meant saying, "God, if everything goes wrong today, You are enough."

## Katie, 20

In high school I was co-valedictorian, on the volleyball team, and did all the right things. I thought being a Christian meant *doing* as much as I could for God, and that He would reward me if I did well. I was so focused on achieving the best grades, the best friends, the best image, that I totally lost sight of what God was trying to tell me: you have to *give up* in order to *gain*.

## Amanda, 20

Growing up, my parents expected a lot from me, thus creating high expectations of my own. I would pour so much time into schoolwork and stress over even the smallest of assignments. Although I still strive for excellence in school, I've come to find that enjoying the process of learning and being proud of my hardest work is more important than perfection on a report card. I'm defined so intricately and perfectly that any sort of affirmation from my schoolwork is insignificant in comparison to the affirmation of my Creator.

## Caroline, 21

I think even girls who have a resume overflowing with accomplishments and leadership roles never feel fulfilled with their achievements, always thinking there is someone better, more talented than they are. If we wake up each day hoping to be better at loving and caring for people, rather than being better at algebra or soccer, we will become more like Christ and not be so consumed with our worldly shortcomings.

## Claire, 22

Looking at me from the outside perspective, you'd think I was the happiest high schooler in the world. I was the varsity cheer captain at a very competitive school, I was the yearbook editor in chief, I made honor roll every semester, and I had a lot of friends. I spent all of my time thinking, *If I can just reach this status, life will be great. One more title and every girl will want to be me.* I didn't realize how destructive this was for me until a good friend and unspoken competitor looked at me senior year and said, "Gosh, Claire, your life is just so perfect. Every mom would dream to have a daughter like you." That was everything I had ever wanted to hear, and yet I felt unbelievably empty. God shook me to my core and revealed to me that I had achieved my "goals," but I felt more insecure and lonely than ever before. I had spent so much time working to the top that I had forgotten to enjoy and savor the life and friendships I already had.

## Hannah, 22

I heard over and over that I could not do anything to make God love me less. Yes, that encouraged me, and that is crazy! But what really stood out to me was when I started believing the truth that there is *nothing* I can do to make God love me more. His love is unconditional. Therefore He loves because we are His daughters and He created us. When you really believe that achievements and talents do not change God's perspective of you, then it gives such freedom to the way we get to live.

## Alyssa, 21

Behind most things I choose to pursue I hear in the back of my mind, *If you do this well—if you win, if you achieve—then you will be good enough and be loved, admired, and praised by others.* In middle school and high school I often placed my worth in being good enough. It is a continuous battle, but it is opposite of the gospel that Jesus shows. He says you don't have to be good enough. He didn't die on the cross once I was cleaned up or had enough recognition from others. He died on the cross and rose when I was still a sinner. I had nothing to offer Him.

## Bailey, 22

Any achievement or talent will fade. However, I am good enough at being *His*. He didn't offer us salvation based on how we perform. We are worth it to Him.

# Why Do I Feel Like I'm Always Being Evaluated?

*by Ali Claxton*

We feel the constant pressure to excel from a very young age. We spend a majority of our lives being evaluated in some form or another by teachers, coaches, bosses, parents, student ministry leaders, and friends. We can hardly keep up with all the expectations—physical, emotional, mental, relational, and yes, even spiritual. There's no escaping it. Every victory increases the pressure to win, and every defeat feels like a permanent mark on our record. It's tough to survive under the weight of expectation.

I teach a group of amazing tenth-grade girls at my church. They are smart, funny, and extremely driven. I listen to them talk about standardized tests, honors classes, college prep, service projects, band competitions, sports, auditions . . . and the list goes on. They spend a majority of every day preparing for, participating in, or recovering from some form of intense activity. And they get evaluated on almost everything they do. Life for them often feels like a never-ending series of tests.

I'm sure you can relate. Your life is likely full of similar opportunities and challenges. You probably experience the same pressure to measure up to a variety of seemingly impossible standards. The desire for excellence can sometimes feel like a demand for perfection, and trying to keep up with such high expectations is an exhausting way to live. If you are going to thrive under pressure, you need to find some rhythm in your schedule and balance for your lifestyle.

Here are a few tips to help you deal with all that pressure:

## 1. Know your strengths.

It's nice to hear people say, "You can do anything you set your mind to." There's a degree of truth to that popular sentiment, and it certainly sounds like a compliment. But just because

you *can* do something doesn't mean you *should*. You've been created with unique talents, personality traits, and passions. Use those to help you determine what opportunities to pursue. When you focus on activities that come naturally to you, you experience consistent growth and a sense of accomplishment even under pressure.

## 2. Set realistic goals.

Striving for perfection in every aspect of your life is impossible. A "no mistakes allowed" kind of attitude will lead to a life of unmanageable stress and future health issues. Yes, you should work hard and do your best at all times, but allowing no room for mistakes also leaves no room for growth. Instead of striving for perfection, make it your goal to pursue excellence. With that perspective, you'll be more willing to try new things and less likely to crack under pressure.

## 3. Don't overcommit yourself.

Cramming your schedule full of activities sets you up for failure. There are only so many hours in the day, and you need to use each one wisely. Everything you say yes to will cost you time and energy. Saying yes to too many activities will eventually force you to sacrifice things such as rest, recreation, quality time with the Lord, and time with family and friends. These are priorities that God uses to rejuvenate your body, encourage your heart, and sharpen your mind. When you trade them for other activities, you'll eventually become weary, uninspired, and unsatisfied.

## 4. Take time to reflect.

Pause and take a deep breath. Slow down every once in a while to reflect on what you've accomplished and make note of where you've grown. When you take time to consider what you've just experienced, you'll find opportunities to celebrate growth and be thankful for your progress. Cultivating an attitude of thankfulness will decrease your stress level and provide a sense of peace.

## 5. Keep your focus on what's most important.

As a believer, your ultimate goal is to glorify God. Letting Him shape your character and use your life to point others to His grace is the greatest ambition of all.

The pressure to succeed will always be there. For the rest of your life, you'll be evaluated based on a variety of expectations. But the pressure doesn't have to crush you. Develop a plan. Determine what goals and opportunities work best for you. Strive to make your attitude and effort honorable in everything you do. And don't lose sight of what matters most.

# WINNING YOUR PARENTS' APPROVAL

*by Pam Gibbs*

## See if you can relate:

- You have nightmares that you forgot your homework.
- Your mom and dad pay more attention to you when you get good grades.
- If the term *school booster* was in the dictionary, your parents' picture would be featured.
- You worry if your grades drop below 96.
- One of your parents got in your coach's face because you don't play enough.
- Your parents are counting on your grades for big scholarships to college.

If any of the descriptions above apply to you, chances are you feel pressure to please your parents. And you're not alone. Lots of other girls (and guys) wish their parents would just back off. Some teens feel like their parents are trying to relive their own teenage years by pushing their kids to do well in school, be popular, make the varsity team (or get the lead role or get that acceptance letter or . . .) sooner than everybody else.

So why do your parents do these things? The answer might surprise you.

## I Didn't Mean To!

I bet you've said this before: "But, Mom, I didn't mean to!" And in all honesty, you didn't mean to. Maybe you spent more money than you promised or missed your curfew because you lost track of time. You know how it feels for something to turn out differently than planned. In the same way, your mom or dad could probably say, "But I didn't mean to pressure her!" Your parents want the best for you. They want you to succeed because they love you. Unfortunately, that deep love for you can come out sideways sometimes—and it feels like pressure. There's a thin line between challenging you and pushing you too far, and sometimes your parents don't know when they've crossed that line.

## Caught Up in the Moment

What's your favorite movie? One on my top-ten list is a thriller. You know, not quite a horror flick but keeps you on the edge of your seat. The first time I saw it, I gripped my husband's hand for so long I left nail marks. I was tense. I was so caught up in the movie, I forgot that it was just that—a movie. I'm sure you've done the same. And so have your parents. This is what they are doing when they sit in the stands at your ball games. They cheer and coach and yell and scream. They go hoarse. They may even be *that* parent—the one *everybody* knows because they're so obnoxious. Their seemingly crazy behavior is most likely because they've lost sight of the fact that it's just a game. It's just a grade. It's just the student council. They know you will be disappointed if you lose, and your parents would do anything to shield you from unnecessary hurt. As a result, they get caught up in the moment and lose perspective.

## *What's a Girl to Do?*

Knowing why your parents are putting so much pressure on you is important. Knowing how to deal with that pressure is even more critical. Try these tips to make the situation more bearable:

1. **Talk with them.** Not at them. After dinner one evening, explain that you're feeling the squeeze to be perfect. Share how you feel. (Yes, *you* start the conversation.) Don't yell in the heat of the moment. Calmly explain how you feel, that you're doing your best (if you really are), and that you would appreciate it if they made fewer comments.

2. **Laugh it off.** If you know for certain that your parents' screaming at ball games is innocent and they're just getting carried away, then blow it off. Joke about it with your friends. "Yeah, that's my mom. Next week she's trying out for the Olympic Scream Team." If you don't make a big deal out of it, neither will anybody else.

3. **Write a letter.** Too anxious to have a conversation? Consider writing a letter. This way you can think more clearly, take time to process what you want to say, edit yourself (so you won't write something you'd regret later), and choose the right time (Christmas Eve is not a good choice).

4. **Redirect the stress.** If you're feeling pressure, take time to release that tension. Like a balloon that pops when you put too much air in it, you'll explode if you don't find ways to lessen the pressure. Go for a run. Listen to music. Take the dog for a walk.

5. **Talk to another adult.** If the pressure is reaching toxic levels (for example, if you want to hurt yourself or you can't sleep), you may need to talk with an adult you can trust, like your pastor or school counselor. They may be able to suggest coping strategies. They may even be willing to help you when you talk to your parents.

The most important thing to remember is this: Your worth is not based on what you do. Your value isn't determined by your parents or anybody else—not even yourself. You are a daughter of God, and for that reason and that reason alone, you have unimaginable worth and value. And no grade or game can take that away.

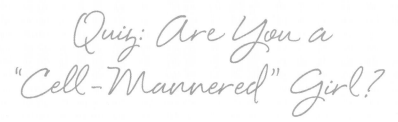

# Quiz: Are You a "Cell-Mannered" Girl?

*by Vicki Courtney*

Cell phones. I bet you can't imagine a day without them. Believe it or not, there are some people who would like to see you try. Cell phones make it possible to stay in touch with your friends and family every minute of every day, but a cell-mannered girl knows when to say hello and when to let it go.

How do you score when it comes to basic cell phone manners? Take the quiz to find out!

1.  **You are at a restaurant with your friends (yes, fast food still counts!), and your phone goes off. It's your best friend who's been at camp for two weeks. You . . .**

A.  answer the phone, scream with excitement, and tell her to come meet you at the restaurant.

B.  tell your friends, "Guys, it's Emily, and she's been at camp for two weeks. I have to get this." You take the call at the table but turn down your volume so as not to disturb others around you.

C.  excuse yourself from the table to take the call in a quieter place, so others can enjoy their meal.

2.  **You are in church, and you forgot to turn off your phone. It vibrates in your bag, indicating you have a text message. You . . .**

A.  check it out and send a quick reply. Besides, it'll make the long sermon go by faster.

B.  check to see who it is. You can call them back when the service is over and you're headed to youth group.

C.  fumble in your bag, grab it, and turn it off quickly. Next time you will leave it in the car so it never happens again. Nothing should distract you or others from giving God the time He deserves.

3.  **You are in a movie theater, and the previews are on. When your phone vibrates, you . . .**

A.  answer it and tell your friend where you are and who you're with. No one likes the previews anyway, right?

B.  send a quick text to your friend telling her where you are. You can trade a few text messages before the movie starts.

C.  turn off your phone. You didn't pay ten bucks to sit in a movie theater and text.

4. **One of your friends is telling you about her painful breakup with her boyfriend. When your phone buzzes, you . . .**

A. tell your friend, "Hang on a sec. I have to respond to this message."

B. check to see who it is while she's talking. You don't plan to reply right away, but you need to check just in case it can't wait.

C. ignore it. Nothing is more important right now than giving this friend your undivided attention.

5. **You're at a party and were supposed to meet one of your friends, but she's not there yet. You . . .**

A. text her while waiting in line to get some food. You text in all caps, "WHERE ARE YOU AND WHAT IS TAKING SO LONG?" You keep texting while filling up your plate and shoving nachos into your mouth.

B. text and ask her when she'll be there. Everyone else in the room is busy talking, and you're feeling left out.

C. make a point to meet new people. If your friend is still not there in another fifteen minutes, you will step outside and send her a quick message to make sure everything is all right.

6. **A friend calls right as you're walking into your favorite coffee shop for a vanilla latte. You . . .**

A. keep the conversation going while standing in line, then tell her to hold on a sec when it's your turn to order. Now that's multitasking!

B. keep the conversation going until it's almost your turn in line. You tell her you'll call her back after you order your drink.

C. tell her you have to go before you step into the store. You don't want to interrupt others with your conversation. Besides, it's too hard to talk, pay, and drink at the same time.

7. **You ride with your mom to pick up your aunt at the airport. Once in the car, she and your mom begin chatting away in the front seat. Your phone rings. You . . .**

A. answer the phone and begin your own little chat-fest.

B. answer the phone, talk for a few minutes, and then tell your friend you need to visit with your aunt.

C. ignore the call and join in on the conversation with your mom and aunt. You can talk to your friends anytime, but your aunt only comes to town once a year. Besides, it's rude to subject others to your conversation when they are trapped in a small space with you and unable to escape.

8. **Your mom is asking you about your day when your phone vibrates with a text message from a friend. She is supposed to text you the times of the movie you're planning to see that night. You . . .**

A. check your phone for the text and send your friend a quick text back. Mom won't mind, right?

B. politely interrupt your mom and tell her you're expecting a text about the movie times. You ask her if it's okay to check the message and reply.

C. ignore the message. It will still be there when you're done talking to your mom.

9. **You are out shopping, and your mom calls just as you are walking into the restroom. You . . .**

A. keep on talking while taking care of business. A few potties flush in the background—but who hasn't heard that before?

B. keep talking right up until it's time to walk into the stall, announcing in the restroom, "I'll call you right back. I gotta go to the bathroom!"

C. don't even think about walking through the bathroom door while still talking on the phone. I mean, it's just wrong on so many levels.

10. **You are at a concert, and your favorite singer and band is on stage playing. You . . .**

A. scream, "This is Jennifer's favorite song!" You dial her number and hold up the phone so she can hear the song.

B. start taking multiple pictures of the band with your phone.

C. enjoy the song and respect the rights of others around you to also enjoy the song. I mean, you all paid big bucks to hear the band live, so it only makes sense to fully enjoy the experience.

**Count the number of A's, B's, and C's you have.**

**If you have mostly A's:** When you look up *rude* in the dictionary, your picture is beside it. Your lack of manners and consideration for others shows that you only care about one thing—*you*! Pray and ask God to help you put others before yourself. More important, back it up with action. You can do it!

**If you have mostly A's and B's:** Yikes. You err on the side of rude when it comes to cell phone manners. Chances are, you're not being rude intentionally and you've never really questioned how your behavior impacts others around you. Make a concentrated effort to think of others and kick your bad habits.

**If you have mostly B's and C's:** Your cell phone manners could use some improvement. If at any given moment you're not quite sure if it's an appropriate setting to talk or text, err on the side of etiquette and practice some restraint.

**If you have mostly C's:** Congratulations! When it comes to cell phone manners, you take the prize. Not many girls your age would fall into this category. Keep up the good work, and maybe others will learn from your example!

# I Deserve It!
## (Dangers of Entitlement)

*by Pam Gibbs*

Your generation is known as the *millennials* because of your link to the year 2000 and beyond. Lately, though, some sociologists and other cultural critics have given you a new title, and you may not like it:

The Entitlement Generation.

Why that negative name? More than ever, teenagers and young adults expect things. Demand things. Some teens think they deserve (fill in the blank with just about anything) because . . . well, because they want it.

Doesn't sound very good, does it?

## What Entitlement Looks Like

Because you were born within the Entitlement Generation, you may not recognize the signs and symptoms. Here are a few indications that you have a problem with entitlement:

- You've asked your mom for money to buy her a Christmas gift.
- You get ticked when someone (parent, teacher, coach) says no.
- You get impatient if the Internet seems slow.
- You don't want to work for anything—grades, clothes, music, etc.
- You expect your parents to fix your problems.
- You don't clean up your messes.
- You want something because "everyone else" has it.
- You think your parents should give you a car on the day you turn sixteen.
- You treat your dad like your personal, bottomless bank.
- You give up easily instead of working hard to achieve your goals.

You may be asking yourself, "So what? What's so bad about feeling entitled?" Good question. Here are a few reasons to ditch this destructive attitude.

1. When you think you deserve everything, you approach God like you would a vending machine. Believing everything revolves around you puts you at the center instead of God. You forget that every good and perfect gift comes from Him (James 1:17). He loves to give good gifts to His children (Luke 11:13), but that does not mean that God is supposed to do whatever you want and give you whatever you ask for.

2. Nothing is guaranteed. Just because you go to college doesn't guarantee a hundred-thousand-dollar salary when you graduate. You'll quickly learn that your salary will increase as your work ethic does. Your boss won't give you a raise just because you showed up.

3. Entitlement creates unreasonable expectations. In college, you can't expect to get an A on a test when you only studied for thirty minutes. After college, you can't expect to get every job you apply for just because you want it. In life, you can't expect other people to overlook your mistakes and poor choices simply because you think you deserve another chance. Which leads to . . .

4. People aren't going to bail you out forever. At some point, your parents will refuse to fix your problems. Your boss will only accept so many excuses. Your professor will give you some grace, but he won't give you an extension just because your computer crashed. Again.

5. Entitlement gives you a bad view of yourself. You'll either begin to think you *can't* do anything for yourself, or you'll think you don't *need* to do anything for yourself. Both of these views are extreme, and they're both wrong. You *can* work hard. And you *can* accomplish great things.

6. You miss out on the joys of work. Believe it or not, achieving a goal feels good. You appreciate that iPhone because you worked extra hours to pay for it. You are proud of that A because you gave up a night out to study.

Part of growing up and becoming a responsible adult is earning your own money, cleaning up after yourself, dealing with disappointment, and working through frustration and roadblocks to get what you want. Otherwise, you'll be living in your parents' basement when you're thirty. And I know you don't want that!

# Bring Out the Best in Others

*by Ali Claxton*

I can still picture their faces in my mind: people who inspired me as a teenager and challenged me to be the very best I could be. They aren't recognizable faces of famous people or well-known leaders. They are ordinary folks with extraordinary influence. People who cared enough to push me beyond my comfort zone and help me become who I am today—family members, coaches, teachers, student ministry leaders, and friends who believed in my talents, challenged my endurance, and encouraged me to see potential I might otherwise have overlooked. On my best and worst days, they helped me recognize my worth in Christ.

That's the amazing thing about how God designed us. We are wired to thrive within community. Yes, it's fun to have people in your life who can make you laugh and tell you what you want to hear, but it's a gift to have people who speak the truth and point you back to Jesus. That's the kind of influence that matters in the long run. That's what we should strive to be in each other's lives.

Cultivating these kinds of relationships takes time and commitment. When we walk alongside people long enough, we discover their strengths as well as the areas where they are most vulnerable to temptation and insecurity. At the same time, we open ourselves up in a way that helps us see our own strengths and weaknesses. As we journey together, we are better able to encourage and challenge one another in our pursuit of Christ.

Proverbs 27:17 says, "As iron sharpens iron, so one person sharpens another" (NIV). Let's think about the process of sharpening iron. Two pieces of iron must connect repeatedly, causing friction that sharpens the edges. This is an intentional process; it doesn't happen by accident. Scripture uses this illustration as a picture of how we should interact with each other. We have the opportunity to sharpen those around us, to help them discover their purpose and potential—and they can do the same for us. This isn't an easy assignment. Nor does it always feel warm and fuzzy. It takes courage to speak truth when someone is headed off course or living recklessly. It takes humility and grace to hold one another accountable in a way that draws us closer to God and each other.

Hebrews 10:24 says, "And let us consider how we may spur one another on toward love and good deeds" (NIV). To spur someone on is to push them forward and remind them that the end goal is worth the struggle. The author of Hebrews challenges us to remain faithful to the people of God and the mission we've been called to. The ultimate purpose for our existence is to make much of Jesus and to love others in a way that reflects His character. We should challenge each other to stay focused on this calling.

Romans 12:9–15 says, "Love must be without hypocrisy. Detest evil; cling to what is good. Show family affection to one another with brotherly love. Outdo one another in showing honor. Do not lack diligence; be fervent in spirit; serve the Lord. Rejoice in hope; be patient in affliction; be persistent in prayer. Share with the saints in their needs; pursue hospitality. Bless those who persecute you; bless and do not curse. Rejoice with those who rejoice; weep with those who weep." There is a beautiful simplicity to this passage. The apostle Paul reminds us that it's a privilege to walk through life with people who share our faith and passion for the Lord. Take care of those God has placed in your life. Pray diligently on their behalf, encourage, challenge, and sharpen them. Be willing to ask tough questions and have uncomfortable conversations when necessary. Be honest; be gracious; be patient. Show up in their lives—not just for the big moments, but in the everyday moments that make them who they are.

Be intentional in how you interact with others, and let your life display the love of Jesus in tangible ways. If you are willing, God will work through you to bring out the best in others. And in the process, He will also bring out the best in you!

Q. *What are some ways you bring out the best in your friends?*

Scan for Video Answers!

# TEN THINGS EVERY COLLEGE FRESHMAN SHOULD KNOW

*by Ashley Anderson*

I remember sitting in my first freshman class at the University of Texas like it was yesterday. I plopped down in a seat in the large auditorium, turned to the friendly looking girl to my right, and introduced myself. We got to talking, and the girl to my left ended up joining our conversation. We exchanged the normal facts (major, hometown, dorm) and then this happened:

Girl to my right: "When I won homecoming queen at my high school—"

Girl to my left: "Wait! I was homecoming queen at my high school too!"

Me: "I was prom queen!"

Awkward silence.

Suddenly I realized things were going to be very different in college. I was no longer the big fish in the small pond of my high school. All the accomplishments I had worked so hard for in high school seemed insignificant. Here I was, sitting in between two other versions of myself, and none of us cared what the others' high school identities were. We were all starting from scratch. I was terrified.

Those first few months of college I longed for someone to know me. Really know me. I wanted my best friend to laugh at my jokes. I wanted my ex-boyfriend (we broke up to go to college) to tell me I was beautiful and special. I wanted my family to hug me and tell me that in no time everyone would realize that I was extraordinary. Basically I wanted everyone who had helped define me during high school to come together and in one collective, rousing cheer tell my entire college campus, "We love Ashley, and you will too!" But since that wasn't possible, I tried to tell funny stories, wear the acceptable college attire, and join the most sought-after organizations. This was all in an effort to show people that I was in fact a *very* fun, talented, smart, unique, and lovable person.

Eventually things got better. And I learned a lot in the process.

I know you aren't in college yet, but if I could give you one piece of advice before you get there, it would be this: in your moments of loneliness, doubt, and insecurity, ask God to remind you how He sees you. His voice is the one that will rise above all the others and calm your heart.

Here are ten things I think every college freshman should know:

### 1. Work hard at school, and find the right balance of study time.

Know your own personality. Will you struggle with studying too much or too little? If you tend toward being a perfectionist, don't let school consume all your thoughts and free time. If you're a procrastinator who's more likely to let your grades slip, remember that school needs to be a priority in order for you to stay there!

**2. *Stop comparing.*** This is a big one! With social media updating you by the minute what all your old high school friends are doing, comparison creeps in quickly. Here's a common scenario: You're lonely one night and trying to decide what to do. You check your Instagram and see that one of your best friends from high school has just posted an epic picture of her having the time of her life at another college. The worst part is that she's attending the college you debated going to instead of the college you're currently attending. You have a moment of panic and consider transferring. Don't believe the hype. We all know that Insta-life is far more glamorous than real life. No one takes pictures of themselves awkwardly meeting new friends or crying in their dorm room. I bet your friend is having similar struggles as you, but you are only seeing the photoshopped version of her night. Invest in your experience, and have confidence that the college you are attending is where God has called you to be.

**3. *Take care of your body.*** This might be the first time you've ever had to exercise apart from organized sports or school activities. Find a gym—many campuses have great facilities—and try to go regularly. This isn't just to avoid the "freshman fifteen." Exercise will help reduce your stress, keep you healthy, and give you more energy.

**4. *Everything is better in moderation.*** The first night in your dorm room, you will probably be thinking, *I'M FREEEE! No parents, no rules!* But you might find yourself crying to your mom on the phone if you spend that first semester overindulging in sleep, food, and Netflix. Before you diagnose yourself with freshman-year depression, consider that you slept fourteen hours last night, then woke up and watched ten episodes of *Gilmore Girls*.

**5. *Make your community a priority.*** You will probably be juggling many different commitments in college: school, activities, dating, sports, keeping up with old friends, and checking in with your family. But investing in new friendships should be at the top of your list. You may never remember what you learned in your freshman-year biology class, but the friend who becomes the maid of honor in your wedding will forever impact your life. Make time for people, including roommates. There are no guarantees on that potluck roommate, but your roommates throughout college can end up being some of your best friends. One classic freshman mistake is to rush into a roommate decision for the following year. Pick your roommates carefully!

**6. Understand friendships take time to build.** I hate to break it to you, but even if you get into your top-pick sorority, you are not going to have twenty new best friends overnight. Friendships take time! Don't be afraid to initiate a hangout with people. Remember that although it may seem like everyone already has friends the first week of class, freshmen are looking and waiting for friends.

**7. Find time to spend in Scripture and prayer.** One great thing about college is you get to manage your schedule. Find a time in the day that works best for you to spend time reading Scripture and praying. Maybe nighttime devotionals are more realistic for you because you're not a morning person. Also, walking to class is a great time to listen to podcasts and worship music, or to pray.

**8. Go to church every Sunday.** Take ownership of your faith apart from your family and join a church near your campus. Find a few friends and start church hunting each weekend. Then pick one, join a small group, and find a way to serve!

**9. Don't go home too much.** You may be living fifteen or fifteen hundred miles from home, but either way, try not to run home every weekend (or to the neighboring college town to see your boyfriend). The comforts of home might be tempting, but every weekend you leave town you are missing important opportunities to plant roots in your college community. I am not saying you should never go home! But the first few months are crucial. During your first semester, commit to staying in town as much as possible and getting out of your comfort zone. Chances are good that both your friendships and confidence will grow, and you will start to feel more at home in college.

**10. Trust God's plan for your life.** Have you ever heard the children's song "He's Got the Whole World in His Hands"? Sometimes the most profound truths are the simplest, and this is definitely one of them. He's got you. And He has promised to never let you go. So when you start to get anxious because every adult in a hundred-mile radius keeps asking you about your major (undeclared) and your dating prospects (which range from zero to complicated), put your trust in God, who already has all the days of your life written in His book (Psalm 139:16).

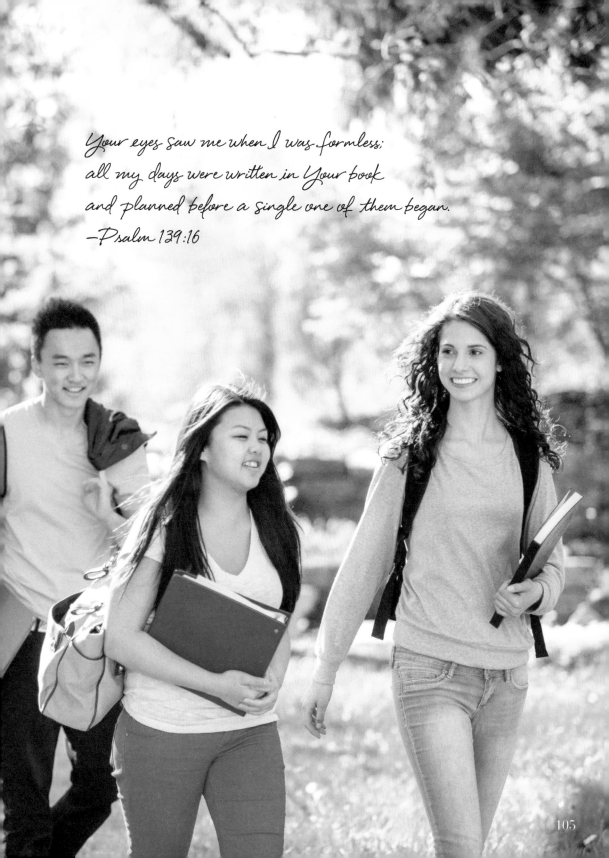

Your eyes saw me when I was formless;
all my days were written in Your book
and planned before a single one of them began.
—Psalm 139:16

# Think This, Not That

*by Tami Overhauser*

Having an identity crisis? Never fear: God has great plans for you! His Word is a constant reminder that His plans are good and He has gifted you to shine for His glory. In the moments when you feel like you don't measure up, think about these words.

"For I know the plans I have for you," declares the LORD, "plans to prosper you and not to harm you, plans to give you hope and a future."—Jeremiah 29:11 NIV

I can do all this through him who gives me strength. —Philippians 4:13 NIV

Trust in the Lord with all your heart, and do not rely on your own understanding.—Proverbs 3:5

So do not throw away your confidence; it will be richly rewarded.—Hebrews 10:35 NIV

Have I not commanded you? Be strong and courageous. Do not be afraid; do not be discouraged, for the LORD your God will be with you wherever you go.—Joshua 1:9 NIV

So we have been sent to speak for Christ. It is as if God is calling to you through us. We speak for Christ when we beg you to be at peace with God. —2 Corinthians 5:20 NCV

Depend on the LORD; trust him, and he will take care of you. —Psalm 37:5 NCV

And whatever you do, in word or deed, do everything in the name of the Lord Jesus, giving thanks to God the Father through him. —Colossians 3:17 ESV

Having gifts that differ according to the grace given to us, let us use them. —Romans 12:6 ESV

But you are a chosen people, a royal priesthood, a holy nation, God's special possession, that you may declare the praises of him who called you out of darkness into his wonderful light. Once you were not a people, but now you are the people of God. —1 Peter 2:9–10 NIV

# Get More Likes

# DO YOU FIT IN?

*by Vicki Courtney*

As a parent volunteer at my son's high school, I once attended a meeting of about three hundred students. The meeting was for a student leadership organization that was given the task of voting for the homecoming theme. I watched with interest as students were given four choices for the theme. Then they raised their hands when their favorite theme was called. A group of about eight or ten girls discussed among themselves which theme they would choose, and when it came time for the vote, they raised their hands in unison for their preferred selection. As they glanced around the room, it became apparent that their choice was not the popular choice; and a few of the girls became visibly uncomfortable and quickly lowered their hands before their vote was counted.

Most teens want to fit in. For the Christian teen, this will be a challenge—especially if fitting in means compromising their faith or values. It's only a matter of time before you are faced with either "fitting in" or "standing strong." Standing strong may mean risking your place in the group. For three handsome teenagers in the Bible, it meant risking their very lives.

Perhaps you remember the account of Shadrach, Meshach, and Abednego in the third chapter of Daniel in the Old Testament. They faced the biggest challenge of their young lives when King Nebuchadnezzar issued a command for everyone to fall down and worship a golden image he had created. This was not your average gold statue. It was ninety feet high! The cue to bow down was the sound of the horn, flute, zither, lyre, harp, pipes, and all kinds of music. Furthermore, the king ordered that anyone who refused to worship the golden image would "immediately be thrown into a furnace of blazing fire" (see vv. 3:4–6).

Shadrach, Meshach, and Abednego refused to bow down and worship the image. The king was notified of their disobedience, and they were summoned to come before him. He gave them one more chance to bow down and worship the idol—and reminded them that disobedient citizens would be cast into the fiery furnace. He further asked them, "What god will be able to rescue you from my hand?" (Daniel 3:15 NIV).

Stop for a minute and think about their dilemma. It is human nature to defend your own life, yet they resisted the temptation to bow down and conform. What a picture to imagine the three men standing amid the music while everyone else hit the dirt, most likely at the first blast of the horn. What a shame they were the only three. Would you have remained standing during the first playing of the song? I hope so. If you think you passed the test, hang on a minute. Now put yourself in their place the second time around. Are you still standing? If it's human nature to want to conform, then it's all the more so to want to *live*.

I love the men's response to the king's command when he gave them a second chance to bow down and worship the golden image.

"Shadrach, Meshach, and Abednego replied to the king, 'Nebuchadnezzar, we don't need to give you an answer to this question. If the God we serve exists, then He can rescue us from the furnace of blazing fire, and He can rescue us from the power of you, the king. But even if He does not rescue us, we want you as king to know that we will not serve your gods or worship the gold statue you set up" (Daniel 3:16–18 NIV).

Now, if that's not radical, I don't know what is. Forget the music and send the orchestra home. No need to play even a chord—these men had made up their minds. They knew their God was capable of rescuing them, even without the foreknowledge of knowing if He actually would. They were prepared to die for God rather than reject Him by bowing down to an idol. Most of us, had we made it through the first song still standing, would have complied with the king after taking one look at the fiery furnace.

King Nebuchadnezzar was so angry with the trio's response that he ordered the fire in the furnace be turned up seven times hotter than normal. In fact, the furnace was so hot that the soldiers who threw the men into the furnace were killed by the flames. Of course, there is a happy ending to the story: Shadrach, Meshach, and Abednego were brought out of the furnace unscathed by the fire. When the king called them out of the furnace, he referred to them as "servants of the Most High God" (Daniel 3:26). By standing up for God in a public way, they were able to give the one true God the glory and honor He deserves. Likewise, we, too, should care more about preserving God's reputation than conforming to the world around us.

Now, I don't imagine you will face the temptation to bow down to a ninety-foot golden statue, but there are plenty of other things that Christian teens willingly bow down to on a daily basis. What about cursing, lying, or gossip? What about drugs, alcohol, or sex? Or viewing inappropriate things on television, the Internet, or in movies? How about joining in with the crowd when it comes to gay marriage, even though it contradicts Scripture? When it comes to the temptation to conform, we need to remember Romans 12:2, which says, "Do not conform to the pattern of this world, but be transformed by the renewing of your mind. Then you will be able to test and approve what God's will is—his good, pleasing and perfect will" (NIV). Are you a Shadrach, Meshach, or Abednego at your school—someone who is more determined to follow God than to follow the crowd?

*Q. How do you and your friends deal with the struggle to fit in?*

Scan for Video Answers!

# The Comparison Game

*by Vicki Courtney*

One time at a speaking engagement, I asked the women in the audience this question: "If you could be any woman in the world, who would you want to be?" I told them I had brought a framed picture of who I would want to be, and I held it closely to me so they couldn't see it. I asked for several volunteers to come up and take a peek at the picture in the frame and see if it was the same person they had picked. One by one, they came up and looked at the picture. One by one, they quickly shook their heads. When the women returned to their seats, I turned the picture around for everyone in the audience to see. It was a mirror! Each volunteer had looked in the mirror and decided the woman she saw was not who she wanted to be. How sad that so few women, if given the choice to be anyone, would want to be themselves.

We're all guilty. We've all compared ourselves to someone else and wished for a moment to be that person instead. I call it the "if only" syndrome. "If only" I had her:

*Cute personality*

*Adorable figure*

*Cool clothes*

*Boyfriend*

*Fashion sense*

*Money*

*Cool stuff*

*Hair*

*Talent*

*Popularity*

I'm going to let you in on a little secret. The truth is, many adults still struggle with the same "if only" list. So what's the cure for the "if only" syndrome? Focusing each and every day on wanting what we have rather than having what we want. I realize this is easier said than done, but with practice it will become a habit before you know it.

For example, if you are dissatisfied with your appearance or body shape, try this daily makeover tip: every morning, stand in front of your mirror and say, "I praise you because I am fearfully and wonderfully made; your works are wonderful, I know that full well" (Psalm 139:14 NIV).

If you often find yourself wishing you had more material possessions or money, memorize these verses: "Don't collect for yourselves treasures on earth, where moth and rust destroy and where thieves break in and steal. But collect for yourselves treasures in heaven, where neither moth nor rust destroys, and where thieves don't break in and steal. For where your treasure is, there your heart will be also" (Matthew 6:19–21).

If you have not yet found your talent, memorize this verse to remind you that God has something very special for you to do someday, even if He has not revealed it to you yet: "For we are His creation, created in Christ Jesus for good works, which God prepared ahead of time so that we should walk in them" (Ephesians 2:10).

One thing I do when I find myself wishing I looked like someone else or had someone else's money, talents, or stuff, is to stop and express my thanks to God over what I do have. If you develop the habit of turning your grumbling into thanks, before long it will become a natural response.

The happiest people are the ones who can honestly say that if given the choice to be anyone on earth, they would choose to be themselves.

# Friends or Followers?

*by Ali Claxton*

We all want to be liked. We want to feel accepted and valued. We want people to notice us and care about the highs and lows we experience. We desire to be connected to others because we were created for community. We crave authentic relationships that go deeper than casual interactions—or social media connections.

With today's technology, it's easy to have a false sense of community. Our culture is obsessed with "friends" and "followers." The more likes or retweets we get, the more popular and fulfilled we feel. Right? But could this obsession with virtual connections lead to a skewed view of what friendship is all about?

Don't hear me the wrong way: there are certainly great aspects to the social media platforms we use on a daily basis. My concern is that when social media is our only community, we trade deep, meaningful relationships for superficial, online interactions.

Pause for a minute and consider your daily social media activity. Do you wake up wondering how many likes you got on the photo you posted the night before? Do you check your accounts multiple times a day to see who has commented, retweeted, or given you a thumbs-up? Do you post or tweet at optimal times when you know the most people possible will see it? If any of the above scenarios fit, you might want to ask yourself why these forms of affirmation are so important to you. And while you're being honest with yourself, consider how social media affects your mood, perspective on relationships, and sense of self-worth.

Acquiring more followers and getting more likes might boost your confidence, but those connections can't change your value. If you're looking for validation through virtual interactions, you will find yourself on a never-ending roller coaster of emotions. What you need more than online followers are real-life friends: people who will speak truth, encourage you, and stand by you on your best and worst days.

It's difficult to consistently challenge and encourage someone from behind a screen. Yes, we can inspire and be inspired through social media, but we can't celebrate victories and struggle through difficulties together without a lasting connection that is strong and authentic. Scripture gives us clear guidance on how we should relate to one another as believers: "Carry each other's burdens, and in this way you will fulfill the law of Christ" (Galatians 6:2 NIV). "Rejoice with those who rejoice; mourn with those who mourn" (Romans 12:15 NIV). "Do nothing out of selfish ambition or vain conceit. Rather, in humility value others above yourselves" (Philippians 2:3 NIV). "Confess your sins to each other and pray for each other" (James 5:16 NIV).

Though it's possible to think about and pray for one another without being physically present, it's difficult to create the kind of relationships that foster sacrificial love without the foundation of a deep connection. We need godly, committed friends who will walk with us through whatever we face on this journey.

We need to be unified as the body of Christ, not merely connected through a form of virtual reality. Your followers on social media are primarily spectators in your life; there may be interaction, but it isn't community the way God intended. We need to walk through life together with other believers, to sit across from each other and talk about the ups and downs instead of simply scrolling through a news feed. We need to be part of each other's lives, not merely an image on a screen.

Let social media be one way of sharing your story with others and keeping up with people you love, but don't let it rob you of the deep relationships God wants you to experience in this life. Instead of striving to get more followers, invest your time in developing deep, Christ-centered connections.

# *Life Unfiltered*

## LIVING AUTHENTICALLY IN A PHOTOSHOP WORLD

*by Pam Gibbs*

If you type in the phrase "photo filters" in the app store on your phone, you will get over four thousand options from which to choose. Some are free, but the ones with more features and options will cost you a little bit. Search on the Internet, and in the "shopping" area alone, you'll be treated to thirty-three pages of possibilities. You can purchase simple software or high-tech programs that cost thousands of dollars—probably more than your first car. You can also buy filters for the camera itself, so you can get that oh-so-perfect shot.

You may think filtering pictures is a twenty-first-century invention, but editing photos dates back to the invention of photography itself. In one of the earliest and most memorable pictures (a lithograph from 1860), Abraham Lincoln is standing by a chair. The picture is of his head, but the body belongs to a Southern politician named John Calhoun. Changes were made to pictures of the Civil War (1864), Adolf Hitler in (1936), and World War II (1945). The 1960s US Hockey Team photo was altered to include people who missed the photo shoot. As techniques advanced, so did the level of expertise in editing. Today, it's almost impossible to detect the real from the fake.

So, why does this little history lesson in photography and editing appear in a teen girls' book? Because it is a reminder that there are a lot of fakes out there—and very little authenticity.

In your social media world, showing the "real you" has been replaced with a different version of you—the polished, zits-removed, take-ten-pictures-and-post-the-best-one, having-fun-with-my-friends—you. Your friends do the same thing. So do politicians, business leaders, political activists, and, of course, celebrities. Think about it: When was the last time you saw a celebrity posting a picture of herself first thing in the morning, fresh out of bed, pre-coffee with a bad case of bed-head? It just doesn't happen. Yes, you may see those in tabloid magazines, but you won't find unflattering pictures on their social media sites.

Growing up in a culture that can edit out the imperfections, you've been taught to believe (and live) a lie: that it's not okay to be flawed. It's not okay to be average or normal. Mistakes are ghastly. Epic. Unimaginable. Don't believe me? Look at your friends' social media. How many of them have posted a picture of themselves without makeup? How many of them mention cleaning up after the dog or taking out the trash? You probably won't find them. Because our culture—especially teen culture—upholds perfection as the standard. Perfect hair. Perfect skin. Perfect posts. Perfect family. Perfect career choice. Perfect, perfect, perfect. Living under that pressure is exhausting and overwhelming. Nobody can live up to that standard 24/7, 365. At some point, you'll buckle under the pressure.

The good news is this: You don't have to live in this polished, plastic, fake world. There is an alternative. It's called authenticity. That's just another way of saying real. Honest. Open. It's the opposite of being fake. Rather than ignoring how you feel and hoping it will go away, you let your actual thoughts and feelings be known—in appropriate ways and at appropriate times, of course.

To do that, though, takes courage. You must be willing to accept the consequences: Not everyone will like you. You will make some people uncomfortable because they don't know how to be real themselves, and your honesty makes them confront their own insecurities. The funny thing is that most of your friends feel the same pressure to be perfect. They are buckling under the weight of living like a filtered picture. They just won't admit it.

Perhaps God has put you in your circle of friends for a reason—to break the plastic shell away and to be willing to show your imperfections. God can use you as an example of what it looks like to be a Christian teenager in today's world. You can show them what it's like to love Jesus and other people, regardless of their struggles or flaws. You can show them the confidence that comes from knowing with certainty that God created you uniquely and marvelously and wonderfully, even with your freckles and height and bone structure. You can demonstrate how to turn to God amid your struggles and insecurities instead of trying to ignore or hide them.

Here's your challenge: the next time you feel unsure of yourself, tell a friend. Don't post some cheesy picture of yourself. Talk about the disappointment you feel over the bad grade you got. Admit that you didn't study enough instead of blaming the teacher. Be honest about the music you like, even if it's modern pan flute music. (Yes, that's a genre of music!) Don't conform to the world's mold. Instead, defy culture. Refuse to be filtered, touched-up, or altered for a better image. Dare to be authentic in a filtered, edited world.

# More Than a Number

*by Rachel Prochnow*

The two friends analyzed the picture, brows furrowed in concentration.

"But do you think it's Instagram worthy?" Her friend grabbed her iPhone and held it close to her eyes, scrutinizing every detail.

"Yeah, for sure. Your hair looks awesome. Plus, that app we found to add makeup makes your skin flawless. You will definitely get at least a hundred likes."

Triumphant, she hit Share.

The next hour was marred by compulsive glances at her phone. She bit her lip, having only gotten twenty-four likes in forty-five minutes—an awful like-to-minute ratio. She turned to her friend. "Should I take it down?" she asked. "I've barely gotten any likes. How many people have already seen it? Do you think people will notice if I delete it at this point?" Her friend fell silent, a sympathetic look crossing her face.

We all have the need to feel loved and accepted. Deep within our souls, we long for validation. We want to be liked, and that longing is normal. Who doesn't want to feel loved or cared about? The rise of social media has made us all highly aware of just how popular we are among our peers. The number of likes you get on a picture, the number of followers you have on Instagram, and the number of views you get on your Snapchat story have enabled us to quantitatively determine our popularity.

I know I've struggled with this.

The scenario I described above is a conversation I've had with my friends countless times. It's only been within the past year that I've realized that the likes I get or the number of followers I have do not determine my worth. In fact, it has zero correlation with my worth.

My worth is found in Christ.
Your worth is found in Christ.
He *never* changes.
He *never* gives up on you.

Isn't that truth so much better than finding your value in the hands of your peers, whose whims change on a daily basis?

The need to be accepted is rooted deep within us. God placed that need within our hearts to draw us to the only One who can fully complete us. Our deepest desire is not linked to a magical number of likes, but rather to one perfect love. Christ is the only One capable of loving you without fail.

Whenever I struggle with my identity I always recall 1 John 3:1: "See what great love the Father has lavished on us, that we should be called children of God!" (NIV). And that is what we are!

Social media can be a really good thing. It's fun to share exciting things happening in your life with your friends. But it's out of balance when it controls you, when you feel compelled to check your phone and monitor the number of likes you receive compulsively.

I challenge you to examine your relationship with social media. The next time you find yourself feeling down when your likes, friends, or followers don't quite measure up to your expectations, reflect on the One whose love has never failed you. Jesus didn't just *like* you: He loved you enough to die for you. But it didn't stop there. The Savior of the universe wants to have a relationship with you.

When that truth is embedded in your heart, does it really matter how many people have viewed your Snapchat story? Liked your picture? Commented on your clever caption? Who really cares?

What do you say? You can turn cartwheels to get a bunch of likes, or you can sit back and dwell on God's perfect love. The choice is yours.

## Never Ever:

- base your identity on how many likes you get or how many followers you have.

- make social media more important than Christ.

- fall into the trap of comparing your social media popularity with others'.

- post pictures or messages that compromise your values.

- forget that you are representing Christ.

# SELFIE-OBSESSED

*by Vicki Courtney*

The selfie-show lasted about five minutes. As I was having my nails done beside the large glass-paned window at the entrance to the nail salon, I noticed her striking a pose in front of the window. Actually, it would have been impossible *not* to notice her. The window in front of the salon was heavily tinted from the outside, so the poor girl was unaware that she had a captive audience of about ten women who had a front row seat on the other side of the glass. The only thing missing was the popcorn. She looked to be about fourteen or fifteen years old, and she held her phone up and flipped her hair while offering a variation of pouts, smiles, and fish lips. She snapped away, picture after picture.

As if it couldn't get any worse, she stopped on occasion to test out a potential pose using the tinted window as a mirror. Then another round would begin. Followed by another. And another. Between each round, she stopped and scrolled through her photos, no doubt looking for the most flattering one to post on social media. There was a hair salon next door, and we quickly surmised she was anxious to show off her new haircut while waiting for her ride. Sure enough, the selfie-show came to an end when her mother pulled up and lightly tapped on her horn to divert her daughter's attention from her photo session.

We had to laugh at the awkwardness of it all, yet similar scenes play out daily in the average teen girl's life. Selfies have become the norm on social media, and some people have struggled to understand this phenomenon. Many argue it is self-absorbed, but even though I'm an old-timer, I see it a bit differently. Sure, some will go overboard and post too many selfies in order to fish for compliments or soothe their ailing sense of self-worth; but others simply want to share a moment with their friends, whether it's a cute new haircut or something else worth celebrating.

Proverbs 27:2 says, "Let someone else praise you, and not your own mouth" (NIV). Sometimes a selfie could be considered a humble brag (or for some, a not-so-humble brag!). Yet behind every selfie, a simple question is really being asked: What do you think of me? It's perfectly normal to wonder what others think of us and to want approval. However, it is unhealthy to base our worth on the opinions of others. The key is discovering the motive behind your selfies. Are you celebrating a moment, or are you fishing for a compliment?

Recently I had a hair appointment, and I thought about my young friend who had unknowingly put on a selfie-show that day at the nail salon. My hair was highlighted, and my stylist had blow-dried it down in a hip new style. It was different from the default ponytail I sported on most days. I knew I would never be able to duplicate the look again, and I wanted to celebrate the moment. Yep—you guessed it. I pulled out my phone, snapped a selfie, and posted it on social media. I'll be honest in saying that it felt good to read the compliments, and certainly I can understand how so many girls are tempted to post too often. However, I knew better than to place my worth at the mercy of a thumbs-up tally of likes and comments. I knew that tomorrow my hair would be back in a ponytail and I would feel just as confident as I had the day before. My worth was already established before I posted the picture. Cute hair or not, I had the only thumbs-up that matters.

When it comes to posting selfies, what is your underlying motive? Are you typically celebrating a moment or fishing for compliments?

### *You might be selfie-obsessed if . . .*

- a high percentage of your pictures are of you and only you.
- you check back often to see how many likes and comments you receive.
- you take the time to scroll through the list of people who liked your selfie.
- you take pictures of yourself on a daily basis (even if you don't end up posting them).
- your friends have harassed you at some point about posting too often.
- you are mindful of the types of pictures and poses that get more attention from guys.
- you find yourself feeling down when a selfie doesn't get as much favorable attention as you had hoped.
- you are in the habit of posing suggestively and posting provocative pictures because of the attention they generate.
- deep down, you care more about what others think of you than what God thinks of you.

*Q. How much do you care about other people's praise?*

Scan for Video Answers!

# Quiz: Are You a People-Pleaser?

*by Pam Gibbs*

**1.  When shopping for new clothes, you think . . .**

A.  *I'm gonna look awesome in this outfit!*

B.  *I wonder if _____ (cool kid) would like it.*

C.  *I saw _____ (cool kid) wear this, so I know it's okay.*

**2.  Your youth minister encourages you to go on a mission trip this summer. You decide to . . .**

A.  go on the trip because you want to help people.

B.  go on the trip because you don't want to look as though you don't care about people.

C.  go on the trip because you're afraid your youth minister will be mad if you don't.

**3.  You've been invited to a sleepover at two different places on Friday night. You decide to . . .**

A.  go with the person who invited you first. That's the fair way to decide.

B.  talk to a couple of friends about the choices to see what they would do.

C.  go to the sleepover at _____'s house because you're afraid she will get really mad and talk about you if you don't.

**4.  You've been dating your crush for several months now. He's told you he wants to do more physically. After all, you love each other. You decide to . . .**

A.  tell him no. You set boundaries before you started dating, and you're not going to change them.

B.  hold off as long as possible, but eventually give in because he's so amazing.

C.  agree to do what he wants because you're afraid of losing him if you don't.

**5.  You've been playing basketball since you could dribble a ball. And you're good. Like, team-captain good. But you're burned-out, and you want to take some time off from the game . . . possibly permanently. You decide to . . .**

A.  take a season off to see if you want to quit, even though your coach and parents might get ticked.

B.  tell your coach you're hurt so he won't get mad at you for taking time off.

C.  play anyway. Your parents are hoping you'll get a scholarship, and you can't let them down.

Now add up your score. If you circled 1, give yourself one point. If you circled 2, then two points. You get the idea. How did you do?

**13 to 15—Danger!** You are making choices based on what others want from you, not on what you want. It's okay to be flexible, but being Jell-O is a poor way to live. People-pleasing will only make you miserable in the end, so do some soul searching to find out why you cave. Remember, God created you uniquely. It's okay to be different from your friends.

**9 to 12—Caution!** Although you don't always worry about pleasing other people, you often fall into the trap of worrying about others' opinions and feelings. It's not wrong to consider others' feelings, but it's not okay to do what other people want because you want their approval. God gave you a brain. Use it!

**5 to 8—Congrats!** You don't let the opinions of others influence your decision making. Your choices are just that—yours. Continue to seek God as you live each day, and you'll make a huge difference in the world around you. Be careful, though. Being your own gal can come across as proud and arrogant, so be willing to give in when it's not a big deal—such as where you go to dinner or who's first in line.

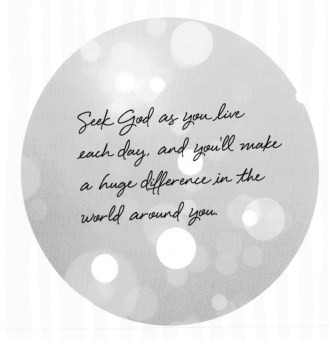

*Seek God as you live each day, and you'll make a huge difference in the world around you.*

# THE 80/20 RULE

*by Vicki Courtney*

Are you a people pleaser? If so, I have a cure that might help. It's called the 80-20 rule, and it's based on this theory: no matter how hard you try to please everyone, roughly 20 percent of those you meet will not like you. Ouch, right? That's got to hurt for the perfectionists who are aiming for a PLS (personal likability score) of 100 percent. I'm not really sure if PLS is really a thing, but if you're a people-pleaser, you know what I'm talking about.

When I was about your age, someone I considered a friend left me off her party list for a big bash she was having over the summer. I was devastated. Everyone in my peer group was invited to the party except for me. I finally heard from a friend that she "could only invite a certain number of people, and Vicki is just an okay friend." I'm pretty sure that translates into "I don't really like Vicki." For several days I sat around and overanalyzed the situation. Was it because we had liked the same guy briefly in fifth grade and he had liked me instead of her? Or maybe it was because I was a cheerleader and she didn't make the first cut in tryouts. Or maybe it was because a group of us had hung out together a few weeks before and she hadn't been included. By the time I had finished making my mental list of possible reasons I had been excluded from her party,

I realized something. I didn't feel any better. It didn't really help to sit around and dwell on a valid reason she didn't consider me a friend. In fact, it only made me feel worse.

I wish I had known about the 80/20 rule back then. Instead of wasting my time over-analyzing the situation and dwelling on one person who fell into the 20 percent, I could have turned my attention to the 80 percent of people who did like me. I'm not saying you shouldn't allow yourself to feel sad when you experience rejection. It's perfectly normal to want to be included and want everyone to like you. Unfortunately, it's not realistic. If I could go back and talk to that sad, confused, younger version of myself, I would tell her to shake it off, find a friend or two in the 80 percent group, and plan your own get-together. I would also caution her from throwing a pity party—because nothing good comes of that. If you sit around dwelling on your disappointment, it robs you of valuable quality time you could be spending with friends in the 80 percent.

I know a guy who started off with a pretty high PLS (personal likability score). He was attentive to the poor, healed the sick, championed the underdog, and put serving others above serving Himself. Who wouldn't like a guy like that? And at first, people did like Him. In fact, they loved Him and flocked to see Him. If He had lived in the era of social media, when your personal likability score is on display for all to see, He would have shattered records with His friend and follower count. This guy was perfect, and I don't say that lightly. I'm talking about Jesus. If ever there was a person who deserved a perfect PLS, it was Him.

Yet even Jesus, perfect as He was, had His share of critics. Some people didn't like how He healed the sick on the Sabbath. Others didn't like how He hung out with those on the fringes of society. Others turned on Him for His bold claim that He had the power to forgive sins. He had masses of followers in His early days, but most of them deserted Him in His final days. Trust me: Jesus was dealing with a far higher percentage of people not liking Him than a mere 20 percent. In fact, many of the people who had been vigilant followers eventually turned on Him and demanded He be crucified. From the beginning of His ministry, He accepted that not everyone He met would like Him. Yet amid that rejection, He didn't sit around and dwell on His low PLS. Nor did He go out of His way to persuade His enemies to like Him. He knew that the approval of man was fickle. Instead, He placed His worth and value in the unchanging love of His Father.

In John 15:18, Jesus said, "If the world hates you, keep in mind that it hated me first" (NIV). Jesus was no stranger to rejection. While it saddens me that Jesus experienced rejection, it comforts me to know that He can relate to what we are feeling when we are rejected. The sting of rejection He felt was so much greater because He gave His very life for those who despised Him. When Jesus hung on a cross and paid the penalty for the sins of mankind, His PLS was lower than most of us will ever understand. In fact, when He was arrested in the garden, even His closest friends had scattered. Peter, one of His most devoted followers, denied he even knew Jesus on three separate occasions. The majority turned against Him, but He didn't focus on that. His mind was on the One who mattered: His heavenly Father, who loved Him no matter what.

The next time you are feeling down because you were left off a party list, or one of the girls you follow on social media doesn't follow you back, or the picture you posted only gets a handful of likes, or you hear that one of the girls in your peer group thinks you're annoying because you sing Taylor Swift songs too loudly in public, or (fill in the blank)—stop and remember the 80/20 rule. Not everyone will like you or want to be your friend. Count your blessings that other people do, and move on. Life is too short to dwell on pleasing the 20 percent.

If you base your worth on the approval of others, you will set yourself up for heartache. Your self-esteem will always be at the mercy of others. Eleanor Roosevelt, the wife of President Franklin D. Roosevelt, once said, "No one can make you feel inferior without your consent." Why give others that much power when it comes to your worth? There is only one vote that matters, and it's God's. Jesus knew that. Do you?

Not everyone will like you or want to be your friend. Count your blessings that other people do, and move on. Life is too short to dwell on pleasing the 20 percent.

# Social Media: The Not-So-Reality Show

*by Pam Gibbs*

"Wow! Look at how many likes she got!"

"I only got ten likes, so I took that one down."

"She's always posting pics with her boyfriend. I'm so jealous."

If you've spent much time on social media, chances are you've said something like this. The cheer captain posts pictures of her weekend away with her family, and you wonder why your family can't be that happy. Or you see a girl's post about her youth group's awesome café-style room, and you think, *If only I could be a part of that church.*

Social media gives you a glimpse into the lives of your friends. You get to see their latest antics with their pet parrot. You watch a video of a friend playing a prank on her brother. A friend talks about her latest project, complete with a how-to. Social media makes it possible to really get the inside scoop on people you know.

Or does it?

On second thought, maybe you're not seeing everything.

When you watch a movie, you see the very best from all of the footage shot in production. Some movies may have two hundred hours of footage with different angles, lights, and tempos, yet you only see a two-hour movie. What happened to the rest?

It got cut. Tossed. You only saw the best of the best.

The same thing happens in social media. You are watching someone else's highlight reel: the very best of their lives; a great day with the fam; fun at the park with a crush; an A in chemistry. What you don't see is everything that got cut: the continual fights between parents; the emotional abuse the boyfriend heaped on last night; the secret longing to be accepted without makeup; the loneliness that sets in when her phone isn't chiming with another notification.

Here's the problem: You and I often compare that other person's highlight reel with our real, everyday lives. And then we get discouraged because there's no way we can ever measure up. That cool family? Forget it. The quarterback boyfriend? Not happening. The no-flab, cellulite-free, perfect body? Good luck with that. Your friends seem so happy, and you feel so . . . ordinary.

The truth is, all of us have highlight reels, and all of us have footage from our lives we'd rather nobody else see. From Billy Graham to Katy Perry, we all have good parts of our lives and not-so-good parts. Nobody lives a perfect life. Nobody. We live in an imperfect world full of imperfect people who make dumb choices they wish they could take back. God has given you—and all of your friends—your own unique, quirky, not-like-anybody-else life. It's a part written just for you. He has put together your gifts and skills and intellect in a way that reflects His glory differently than anyone else does. And you have your own struggles too. Struggles that nobody else sees. Just remember, though, that everybody else has struggles . . . struggles that you will never see.

The next time you wander across your friends' posts, remember this: everyone faces their own battles that you know nothing about. Just thank God for His grace and His help in living out the script He has given you to play. And play it with passion.

# Back in The Day

THE LADIES' HOME JOURNAL, APRIL 1890

## If You Want to Be Loved

Don't find fault.

Don't contradict people even if you're sure you are right.

Don't be inquisitive about the affairs of even your most intimate friend.

Don't underrate anything because you don't possess it.

Don't believe that everybody else in the world is happier than you.

Don't conclude that you have never had any opportunities in life.

Don't repeat gossip, even if it does interest a crowd.

Don't go untidy on the plea that everybody knows you.

Don't be rude to your inferiors in social position.

Don't over- or under-dress.

Don't express a positive opinion unless you perfectly understand what you are talking about.

Don't get in the habit of vulgarizing life by making light of the sentiment of it.

Don't jeer at anybody's religious belief.

Don't try to be anything else but a gentlewoman—and that means a woman who has consideration for the whole world and whose life is governed by the Golden Rule, "Do unto others as you would be done by."

# Pearls and Pigs

*by Vicki Courtney*

With the rise in popularity of texting and social networking sites like Twitter and Snapchat, many teens now type things they would never in a million years say to someone's face. Chances are you have experienced the awkwardness of having a guy say something to you that is sexually inappropriate. I've seen comments posted by guys on girls' pictures that would make your grandmother blush. While I am disappointed in the guys, I can't help but wonder why these girls allow guys to talk inappropriately to them. Are they so desperate for attention that they are willing to settle for the wrong kind of attention? Some girls may even be flattered by the comments, because otherwise they would have deleted them. I saw one Christian girl, who had listed the Bible as a favorite book in her profile, with numerous sexually inappropriate comments posted on her page. One guy friend jokingly described in graphic detail a sexual act he wanted to perform on her. I know, I know—it's all in jest. But it's not funny.

Some guys will test a girl's limits to see if she will tolerate sexual banter. It's similar to what happens when a substitute teacher shows up and the class tests the boundaries to see what they can get away with. If the rules are loose, there's a good chance that the class will take advantage of the teacher. On the other hand, if the teacher takes charge from the beginning and has clear expectations, it is less likely that boundaries will be crossed. Likewise, girls who allow guys to speak to them inappropriately have provided a welcome mat for future inappropriate comments.

When my daughter was a teen, we talked often about boundaries and where to draw the line when it comes to sexual banter. I suggested that should a guy ever speak to her in an inappropriate manner, she should firmly tell him, "Do not talk to me that way ever again." Should he continue, I told her to cut off all future communication with him. He is not worth her time. I know this sounds like harsh advice, but if you take a look at Ephesians 5:4, it doesn't give any wiggle room for sexual banter and cautions God's people against participating in "obscene stories, foolish talk, and coarse jokes" (NLT).

Our conversation brought to mind a passage of Scripture where Jesus preached to a crowd on a mountainside. It starts in Matthew 5 and ends three chapters later. I know you are probably not fond of long sermons, but this one is well worth reading in your spare time. In fact, Matthew 7:28 says, "When Jesus had finished this sermon, the crowds were astonished at His teaching." Consider it a sort of pep talk on how to live life to the fullest. He covered everything from loving your enemies (ouch) to not obsessing over what you will wear (double ouch). But tucked away in the passage is this priceless bit of advice: "Do not give dogs what is sacred; do not throw your pearls to pigs. If you do, they may trample them under their feet, and turn and tear you to pieces" (Matthew 7:6 NIV).

You don't have to search long on social media to find examples of insecure Christian girls who are throwing their pearls to pigs, slopping in the mud with the swine rather than guarding their priceless pearls in a treasure chest. You are worth more than that. Remember that if a guy crosses the line with sexual banter, don't stick around for the mud bath. Save your pearls for a prince, not a pig.

*Do not give dogs what is sacred; do not throw your pearls to pigs. If you do, they may trample them under their feet, and turn and tear you to pieces.*
*—Matthew 7:6*

# THE TRUTH ABOUT PRINCE CHARMING

*by Vicki Courtney*

When my son was in high school, he experienced torture of the worst form. He and his friends made plans to attend a movie, which was not unusual—unless, of course, you let the girls choose the movie. One night he was forced to endure two hours of the latest chick flick, and when he got home, he wore a dazed and confused expression—similar to the kind you get when someone tells you a really lame joke and attempts to explain the punch line over and over again as they wait expectantly for you to laugh. Here's my son's review of the chick flick: "Mom, I just didn't get it. The whole movie led up to this guy and girl getting together at the end. He goes through all this stuff to prove his love for her, and then he has to chase her down at the end to tell her. Give me a break. Like a guy would really go to all that trouble to tell a girl he likes her. Trust me: any girl that puts a guy through all that automatically goes on the psycho list."

Bless his confused and insensitive heart! I then patiently explained that the price of a movie ticket was a small price for a girl to pay to view the world as it should be. The fairy tales, the chick flicks, and the romance novels cater to a woman's desire to be noticed, pursued, rescued, and eventually won over by the world's most charming man. The perfect man will solve all of life's problems and bring us the happiness we long for—a happiness that won't come until or unless we find him. Only then will we crack the code to true love. If and when we find him, we will be forever changed—or so we are led to believe.

Ever notice how the chick flicks always end on an unrealistic high note? With a kiss, time stands still. And there it ends. We are left to imagine the happiness that follows. Of course the couple gets married, and she stares adoringly at him. They go on picnics in the park, and she stares adoringly at him. They run hand in hand on the beach, and she stares adoringly at him. Yeah, right! Can you imagine what would happen if the movie continued with a more realistic picture? He forgets to put down the toilet seat, channel surfs, belches, scratches, and, even worse, eats the last Double Stuf Oreo and leaves the crumbs on the counter for her to clean up. Do you think she's still staring adoringly at him? Doubtful.

What? You don't like reality? Well, that's the reason we have chick flicks—so we can get our romance fix and return to reality. This is not to say that marriage is never romantic. A good marriage will have its moments of romance, but even the best of marriages won't emulate the chick flicks.

These movies do get one thing right. We crave a brand of love that is lasting, perfect, and unfailing. Believe it or not, God placed that craving in our hearts. Proverbs 19:22 says, "What a person desires is unfailing love" (NIV). God's ultimate goal was for our craving for perfect love to lead us to the only One who can offer it—Jesus Christ.

One of my favorite passages of Scripture is Ephesians 3:17–19. It says, "Christ may dwell in your hearts through faith. And I pray that you, being rooted and established in love, may have power with all the Lord's holy people, to grasp how wide and long and high and deep is the love of Christ, and to know this love that surpasses knowledge—that you may be filled to the measure of all the fullness of God" (NIV).

The word *filled* in this verse is derived from a Greek word *pleroo*, which means to "complete" or "fill to the brim."[1] Dream about Prince Charming all you want, but don't be fooled. There is not a guy out there who will be able to complete you.

Don't fall for the fairy tale any longer. No mortal man can offer you a brand of love that will quench the desire in your heart to be loved perfectly and completely. No one can love you with the love of God. Only when you allow Jesus Christ to take His rightful place in your heart will you find true love, and that's no fairy tale.

. . . And then she met her one true Prince and lived happily ever after. The End.

***Source:***

1. James Strong, *The New Strong's Concise Dictionary of the Words in the Greek Testament and the Hebrew Bible* (Bellingham, WA: Logos, 2009), s.v. "filled."

# WISE WORDS FROM COLLEGE GIRLS

*by Ashley Anderson*

We asked a group of college girls to share their thoughts on struggles they faced at your age and what they've learned in the years since. Here's what they had to say about trying to win approval from others. . . .

### Alison, 21

I cared a lot about what people thought of me in high school, which eventually led to drinking and trying drugs on the weekends with the popular kids. I felt like I needed to be accepted by them, so I did whatever they did, even when I didn't want to. It wasn't worth it—I ended up being someone I wasn't and felt worse than before.

### Katie, 20

Caring too much what others think is still my biggest struggle. I know that I am doubting God and not believing that He is enough for me. What has made me stronger in this area over the past few years is becoming stronger in my faith, pouring out and being poured into, trusting that God cares about me more than anyone ever could.

### Amanda, 20

I am a quiet person, and for a long time I thought that was a fault. Because of this, I've always had a hard time standing out in a crowd. High school, therefore, was pretty hard at some points. I felt the need to change myself and force an extroverted personality in order to impress my classmates. Boys didn't notice the girl who didn't say anything. I began to feel like my "normal" self would change depending on who I was with or where I was. This was exhausting. Although I may not thrive in large groups, I find so much joy in getting to know people one-on-one and have made my best friends this way. When I was able to release my mask, I felt a freedom that gives me so much joy. A joy in knowing that I'm loved for myself.

### Caroline, 21

In high school, I spent a lot of energy trying to convince people I didn't care what anyone thought of me—that I was a free spirit unafraid to make a fool of myself—when I actually cared a lot. My freshman year I concocted a long Christmas list derived solely from what the other girls at school wore, but I still always felt less cool, less pretty, less "in." I feel like I really began to let go of this desire when I grew close with a group of girls in college who loved the Lord and knew how to build one another up. I didn't feel like I needed approval from anyone anymore because they appreciated the quirky or different things about me and knew how to remind me that God did too.

### Claire, 22

I hit a breaking point in high school when I realized that I had worked to impress and please others for so long that I forgot who I really was. Like really deep down, who was I? It took some real searching for me to figure out the answer to that question. I had to recognize that I will never be the nicest, prettiest, smartest, most fun girl in a crowd. At least not by my own tough standards. What matters most is that the Lord considers me worthy of His love and praise. For so long He had been reaching His arms out to me, but I was constantly turning my back on Him to reach my arms into a rushing crowd of people. I was looking for what I already had in front of me. The Lord is faithful, and true freedom is found in loving yourself the way God created you to be.

### Taylor, 21

The amount you nitpick and obsess over the things you don't like about yourself is far, far greater than what anyone ever even notices about what you consider your faults. Give yourself the grace Jesus gives you.

### Bailey, 22

Once we fully believe that we are loved, accepted, and fully known by God, then we can live in freedom! This is easier said than done. We love what we can see. We want the people around us to like us and love us for who we are. However, their acceptance isn't enough to satisfy. We crave the love and acceptance from the one who made us. The one we can't physically see. What's even crazier is that He freely offers that to us! We have to truly fight to believe that, in order to be free from the burden of wanting to please others. We have to have faith that He loves us unconditionally and deeper than we can fathom.

# Beware of the Hook-Up Trend

*by Vicki Courtney*

I had a roommate in college who was the chaplain of her sorority. She was in charge of opening the meetings in prayer and organizing small-group Bible studies. When her birthday rolled around, I set out in search of a Christian music tape (no such thing as digital downloads yet!) that she'd told me she wanted. I was not a Christian at the time, and

I recall the awkwardness of walking into a Christian bookstore. My roommate's faith was a mystery to me. I was searching for meaning and purpose in my life, but I was resistant to embrace Christianity based on some unfortunate episodes of hypocrisy I had witnessed in my earlier years. I was watching her closely to see if she was any different

from some of the Christians I had known in the past who couldn't seem to match their walk with their talk. Unfortunately, I didn't have to watch long. One morning we were talking about a date she had been on the night before with a guy she had met at a party. She had been really excited about this date, so I couldn't wait to hear about the details.

She gave me way more details than I ever wanted to know. She told me that it was very clear by the end of the date that he wanted *something*. She shrugged it off and said, "So I gave him what he wanted so he would leave me alone. We didn't have sex, but, you know . . ." I was shocked. I would never do such a thing, yet she was the Christian!

In my day, behavior like that was considered unacceptable. In fact, we had a name for girls who had one-night stands. Unfortunately, what my roommate did is common in teen culture today. Girls and guys "hook up" and mess around sexually. Some go all the way, and others come close. Many who have been brainwashed by television, movies, music, and fashion magazines shrug it off as no big deal. There was even a study done among college women that determined dating has pretty much been replaced by "hooking up." Girls interviewed in the study claimed that guys have come to expect hookups.

Many girls expressed frustration that very few guys will work up the nerve to ask a girl out on a date, pay for the date, and behave as a perfect gentleman by expecting nothing in return at the end of the date—especially when so many girls are willing to hook up for free, no strings attached. The study also revealed that hookups were taking an emotional toll on the girls. In light of the culture's cry for sexual freedom and the right to have sex without obligations, girls couldn't seem to rationalize it away like the guys.

One reason for this would be the hormone oxytocin. Oxytocin acts as a messenger hormone that is sent from a woman's brain to the uterus and breasts to induce labor and let down milk after a baby is born. But here's where it gets interesting. It has been discovered that oxytocin is also released during sexual activity. Oxytocin is the hormone that not only bonds mother and child, but also connects husband and wife. It has also been discovered that oxytocin increases trust between the woman and her partner. Trust builds confidence that the person you have now "bonded" with will be there for you—always and forever.

Psychologist Jess Lair of Montana State University described the complex connection that takes place during sexual intercourse, saying,

"Sexual bonding includes powerful emotional, psychological, physical, and spiritual links that are so strong that the two people become one, at least for a moment. Sexual intercourse is an intense, though brief physical bonding that leaves indelible marks on the participants . . . To believe one can walk away from a sexual experience untouched is dangerously naïve."[1]

In light of the information regarding oxytocin, now consider God's design for marriage when He says, "A man leaves his father and mother and is united to his wife, and they become one flesh" (Genesis 2:24 NIV). Other references to the act of sex bonding husband and wife as "one flesh" occur in Matthew 19:5, Mark 10:8, and Ephesians 5:31. But what if sex occurs with someone who will not become a person's spouse? Would that same act of bonding occur? Consider 1 Corinthians 6:16, which says, "Do you not know that he who unites himself with a prostitute is one with her in body? For it is said, 'The two will become one flesh.' " It should come as no surprise that the scientific discovery of oxytocin supports God's design for sex: it is reserved for a husband and wife in the confines of marriage. God created oxytocin as a "glue" to bond mother and child, husband and wife. Sex outside of marriage short-circuits God's design for sex, triggering a premature trust that likely won't last.

God created sex to be a beautiful expression of love between a husband and wife. When sex or sexual activity is practiced outside of marriage, it will always lead to emptiness and confusion. Shame may not follow immediately, but rest assured, it will follow. We are not wired to hook up casually without suffering emotional consequences. Many girls will hook up as a means to get the attention they desperately crave from guys.

Christian girls should never settle for this kind of negative attention. First, it is sin, and sin will never fill the void in your heart. Second, you are a child of the King and set apart for great things—not casual one-night stands. Your worth should come from knowing you are loved beyond measure by the God of the universe. Make it a habit to bask in the glow of His perfect love. You deserve respect, but first you must respect yourself.

***Source:***
1. "The Benefits of Chastity Before Marriage." www.foreverfamilies.net/xml/articles/benefitsofchastity.aspx.

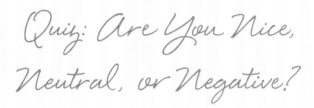

# Quiz: Are You Nice, Neutral, or Negative?

*by Tami Overhauser*

Did you know that the Golden Rule is actually in the Bible?

*Do to others what you would have them do to you.*
*—Matthew 7:12 NIV*

It's not always easy to uphold, though, is it? Awhile back I came up with a sliding scale for my teenage daughters so they could gauge how they were treating others. Take our quiz and see where you land. Are you nice, neutral, or negative when relationships get sticky? I bet you'll find, like we did, that there is always room for improvement.

**Scenario #1. Your best friend starts to pull away from you and spend time with a different group of girls at school. The problem is, you still see her at youth group, where she acts as though nothing is wrong. You . . .**

A.  enjoy the time you have together, showing her kindness and true friendship. Pray about a possible time to talk about it.
B.  take part in some group activities with her at church but don't act overly friendly.
C.  snub her, sitting as far away as possible. Maybe even get the church group to turn against her. After all, that's what she did to you.

**Scenario #2. You see that not-so-nice girl sitting alone at lunch, and she seems to be crying. You . . .**

A.  know that no one should be alone at a time like this! You go immediately to sit with her and see if she is okay. Who knows? This could even be an open door to show her God's love.

B.  ask around the lunchroom to see if she is okay. Secretly you are concerned and hope it's nothing serious.

C.  don't even look in her direction and say to your friends, "She probably deserved whatever happened."

**Scenario #3. Your boyfriend is spending all his free time with his guy friends. It's been weeks since you've had some one-on-one time. You . . .**

A.  find a good time for both of you to talk (not text) about it. Tell him how you really feel and that you miss spending time with him. Ask him how he feels too.

B.  act distant, but when he asks about your behavior, say, "Nothing's wrong."

C.  decide that the next time he is free *you* will be busy with *your* girlfriends and show him how it feels.

**Scenario #4. Your older sister plans to take you to dinner and a movie, but at the last minute her boyfriend calls, and she ditches you. When she comes home she wants to tell you all about her date. You . . .**

A.  have had time to pray about it and realize you really can't blame her; you might have done the same thing. You sit down and say, "Tell me everything!" You really *do* want to hear all about it.

B.  pretend to have already gone to sleep. You will deal with this tomorrow.

C.  wait up for her and give her a piece of your mind. Who does she think she is?

**Scenario #5. While working in a group on a history project, a classmate mentions she has never been to church and her family does not believe in God. A few other members snicker, and it's obvious she is the only one. You . . .**

A.  lean close to her and say, "You should come with me sometime!" (You make sure to follow up before Sunday.)

B.  look down at your study guide and awkwardly change the subject.

C.  laugh as well and say, "Wow, I've never met anyone who doesn't believe in God!"

**Scenario #6.** After playing on the varsity soccer team last year, you were demoted to junior varsity this season despite your hard work at tryouts. You . . .

A.   take a day or two to be disappointed, then give it your all. You are thankful to be playing, and this team needs you! Who knows what the year will bring.

B.   sulk around a bit, letting it affect your performance, but smile politely when people congratulate you.

C.   decide to quit! It's varsity or nothing for you. Then bad-mouth the coaches and other players. It's all their fault anyway.

*Mostly A's. Nice.* Congratulations—you've got this down! You know the importance of kind words and gestures and just how to make someone feel valued. You are that friend who loves at all times. Keep up the good work. Attitude is everything.

*Mostly B's. Neutral.* You know the old saying, don't you? "If you don't have anything nice to say, don't say anything at all." A neutral stance often keeps the peace, which can be good. Certainly, if you are feeling negative, neutral is a good alternative; but be careful you don't hold negative feelings toward someone in your heart or miss an opportunity to show kindness. Perhaps ask God how you might go the extra mile and move from *neutral* to *nice* next time.

*Mostly C's. Negative.* Relationships can be hard, but that doesn't mean *we* need to be! Sometimes we get so wrapped up in our own lives that we fail to see the needs of others. Remember that God has called us to love others, even when they don't seem loving or loveable. Ask God to give you a new love for others and to help you treat them the way you would want to be treated. Think how different our world would be if everyone did this. Just a little tweaking of the ol' attitude, and you will move way past neutral and all the way to nice!

You have heard that it was said, "YOU SHALL LOVE YOUR NEIGHBOR and hate your enemy." But I say to you, love your enemies and pray for those who persecute you. —Matthew 5:43–44 NASB

Do not repay evil with evil or insult with insult. On the contrary, repay evil with blessing, because to this you were called so that you may inherit a blessing. —1 Peter 3:9 NIV

So whatever you wish that others would do to you, do also to them. —Matthew 7:12 ESV

A friend loves at all times. —Proverbs 17:17

# *PICTURE THIS*

*by Anonymous*

"Just one picture. Puhleeeeese. I won't show it to anyone." It was the text that changed everything. My boyfriend and I had been dating for nearly a year, and things had gotten comfortable. Way too comfortable. He was my first boyfriend, and I'm not sure what I liked more: him or simply the idea of having a boyfriend. Most of my friends had already had a boyfriend or two, so it was nice to know I had been noticed. We enjoyed the same things, and most importantly, we shared the same faith. In fact, we met on a summer mission trip, and

I loved his heart for helping the less fortunate. We stayed up late talking one night on the trip about our desire to change the world for Christ. After the trip, we started spending more time together, and eventually we decided to date. My parents even liked him and told family members he was "a nice, young, Christian man." Originally, he was.

In all fairness, I didn't cave in right away. As our relationship got more comfortable, he began to toss out comments here and there about wishing he had "a picture." He would guilt me and say most of his friends had nude pictures of their girlfriends. Sadly, I knew he was probably telling the truth. In the beginning I was able to ward off his requests by changing the subject or even feigning an interruption that would provide me with a quick way of escape. Sometimes he would even apologize the next day and tell me he had asked God to forgive him. I knew this kind of thing was a struggle for most guys, but I thought I could be strong enough for the two of us when he was experiencing a moment of weakness or temptation.

Then one day he wore me down. It was late at night, and we'd been texting for a while. I told him I was tired and wanted to get ready for bed. Our conversation took a turn, and he texted, "Send me a picture of that—the 'getting ready' part." At first I didn't know what he meant, but then it hit me. "C'mon, just one pic, and I promise I'll leave you alone." As I slipped out of my shirt and went to put on a flimsy tank, I aimed the camera at my bathroom mirror and snapped a quick picture. I knew it was wrong, but at the same time, I was flattered that he was giving me so much attention. Even though I felt an immediate stab of regret, it was also mixed with a flash of exhilaration. It was nice to know I was desirable. For the first time I understood my youth minister's warning to be on guard—because "sin is often disguised as fun."

That picture changed everything. Gone were our deep conversations about our hopes and dreams for changing the world. After I sent the picture, after I gave him a sneak peek of the outside, he no longer seemed to notice the girl I was on the inside. Of course, he wasn't satisfied for long with one picture. He wanted more—more pictures and more physical things, if you know what I mean. I eventually grew weary of telling him no and rebuffing his advances, so I prayed and asked God to give me enough strength to end the relationship. Shortly thereafter, he asked for another picture; and when I refused, he followed with a heavy dose of manipulation. "My friends get pictures from their girlfriends all the time. . . . It's not that big of a deal. . . . Don't you love me? You know I would never show them to anyone, right?" Finally I had had enough. I'd reached my limit and told him it was over. I immediately blocked his number so I wouldn't cave in when he texted. It was hard, but I reminded myself that he wasn't the same guy I had originally fallen for.

A week later, as I walked by a group of his friends at school, one of them looked right at me, smiled, and said, "Nice." And I knew. When I confronted my ex, he denied showing anyone the picture, but he eventually admitted that "one of his friends had gotten his phone, found the picture, and sent it out to a few people without his permission." Yeah, right. Shame washed over me as I imagined what my friends in the youth group would think of me if they found out. Or even worse, my parents, my pastor, or—ugh—even my grandparents. Most of all, I wondered if I could ever face God again. I was so ashamed.

In the days that followed, I lost sleep and struggled with anxiety. It was torture going to school each day and wondering who had seen the picture. Finally I told my youth minister's wife because it felt so good to confess the sin to someone. She encouraged me to tell my mom in order for steps to be taken to ensure the picture didn't spread any further. I resisted at first, but I knew it was the right thing to do. It was one of the hardest things I've ever done, but I'm glad I did it. My parents were disappointed, but they were quick to extend grace and remind me of God's forgiveness. They both admitted to having their own regrets at my age and needing that same grace, which has helped me move on.

As painful as it's been, God has used the experience to deepen my faith and remind me of His unconditional love and forgiveness. My youth minister's wife shared a Bible verse that I've memorized, and when shame pays me a visit, I focus on it. The verse is Psalm 103:12, and it says, "As far as the east is from the west, so far has He removed our transgressions from us." Do you know how far apart the east is from the west? The two points never meet. His forgiveness is literally never-ending. The verse is a beautiful reminder that when God sees me, He doesn't see my sin.

If you know someone who has been in my shoes, or maybe you can personally relate, memorize, or pass along that verse. Why dwell on *that* picture, when you can remember instead the beautiful picture of God casting your sins away? Gone. Forgiven. Never to be remembered. That is the only picture worth remembering.

As far as the east is from the west, so far has He
removed our transgressions from us. —Psalm 103:12

# Think This, Not That

*by Tami Overhauser*

**W**hether online or offline, relationships can be difficult. Fortunately, God has given us some guidelines when it comes to managing our friendships. We don't have to fall into the trap of caring too much about what other people think of us.

*Do nothing out of rivalry or conceit, but in humility consider others as more important than yourselves. —Philippians 2:3*

*Let the words of my mouth and the meditations of my heart be acceptable in your sight, O LORD, my rock and my redeemer. —Psalm 19:14 ESV*

*Search me, God, and know my heart; test me and know my anxious thoughts. —Psalm 139:23 NIV*

*But, "If people want to brag, they should brag only about the Lord." —2 Corinthians 10:17 NCV*

Accept one another, then, just as Christ accepted you, in order to bring praise to God. —Romans 15:7 NIV

Each one should test their own actions. Then they can take pride in themselves alone, without comparing themselves to someone else. —Galatians 6:4 NIV

Do not think you are better than you are. —Romans 12:3 NCV

A friend loves at all times. —Proverbs 17:17

You have heard that it was said, "Love your neighbor and hate your enemy." But I tell you, love your enemies and pray for those who persecute you. —Matthew 5:43–44 NIV

If it is possible, as far as it depends on you, live at peace with everyone. —Romans 12:18 NIV

Treat people the same way you want them to treat you. —Matthew 7:12 NASB

# The Truth of The Matter

# WHEN "GOOD" ISN'T GOOD ENOUGH

*by Vicki Courtney*

How many of you have heard someone say, "As long as you're a good person, you'll go to heaven"? I'm pretty sure I said it myself before I became a Christian. Years ago I did an informal survey at an event for middle and high school girls and asked the question, "What does it take to go to heaven?" Most of the girls at the event were Christians, so I couldn't believe it when most of the answers they turned in related to good deeds and "being good."

The bottom line is that we will never be good enough to earn God's favor. I remember an example that a speaker used at an event years ago that really drove the point home for me. He said to imagine there were three men who claimed they could successfully jump across the Grand Canyon. One was just an average guy. The second guy was athletic. The third guy was an Olympic gold medalist in the long jump. The first guy took off running to make the jump, made it about ten feet out, and plunged into the canyon. The second guy was more confident, knowing he was in good physical shape. He took off running, made it out about fourteen feet, and plunged into the canyon. The third guy was the most qualified as an Olympic long jump champion. If ever there was a person who could jump the Grand Canyon, he was the one. With confidence he took off running and made a record jump of thirty feet, then plunged into the canyon. The average width of the Grand Canyon is ten miles, which converts to about 52,800 feet. It didn't matter how much the Olympic long jumper had trained or how many feet he could jump—in the end, he would come up about 52,770 feet short.

It is the same when it comes to earning our way to heaven based on good deeds. Isaiah 64:6 says, "All of us have become like one who is unclean, and all our righteous acts are like filthy rags" (NIV). It doesn't matter how good we are; we can never match the purity and goodness of God. God cannot be in the presence of any sin, so if you have sinned even once (and trust me, you have), you cannot be in His presence. Of course, that is what the good news is all about. Jesus Christ came to bridge the gap between sinful man and a Holy God. The Bible tells us that there is no forgiveness without the shedding of blood (Hebrews 9:22). When Jesus died on the cross, the shedding of His blood became the sacrifice for our sins. Those who believe in Jesus Christ acknowledge that He has paid the penalty for their sins, and they can stand righteous before God. God does not see their sins because they are washed clean by the blood of Christ.

Scripture gives us this assurance: "God makes people right with himself through their faith in Jesus Christ. This is true for all who believe in Christ, because all people are the same: Everyone has sinned and fallen short of God's glorious standard, and all need to be made right with God by his grace, which is a free gift. They need to be made free from sin through Jesus Christ. God sent him to die in our place to take away our sins. We receive forgiveness through faith in the blood of Jesus' death. This showed that God always does what is right and fair, as in the past when he was patient and did not punish people for their sins. And God gave Jesus to show today that he does what is right. God did this so he could judge rightly and so he could make right any person who has faith in Jesus" (Romans 3:22–26 NCV).

While the Bible tells us to seek to please God and do good works, there is no way to do enough good works to reach God on our own. We need help to make it across the Grand Canyon of sin. It doesn't matter how "good" we are; we will always fall short. Only Jesus can help us make the jump.

Most other world religions are based on humankind trying to be "good enough" to earn God's favor. Christianity is a beautiful picture of a loving, holy God who reaches down to us in our sinful state and says, "I'll take you just as you are." The amazing thing is that once the reality of that kind of unconditional love begins to sink in, we are motivated to do "good" as a result of the gratitude we feel in our hearts.

You will never be able to jump across the Grand Canyon of sin, but Jesus has already done it for you. And He's waiting on the other side.

# How God Feels About You

*by Ali Claxton*

Do you ever wonder how God feels about you? Does He think about you? Is He proud of you? Does He get frustrated with you when you disobey? Is He moved by your tears? Does He cheer when you succeed or feel disappointed when you fail?

These are honest questions that we've probably all considered at some point in our lives. Our tendency as human beings is to assume that God responds to people and circumstances the same way we do. When we mess up, we assume God is frustrated or disappointed in us because that's how we feel. When we experience success, we naturally think our heavenly Father must be beaming with pride over our accomplishments. But before we can really understand God's feelings for His children, we need to get to know His character.

God is not like us. He doesn't experience emotional ups and downs or mood swings. As fallen people, our feelings are influenced by intentions and expectations of our imperfect hearts and minds. Though we are made righteous through a relationship with Christ, we still struggle with our flesh—the sinful thoughts and desires of this life. Because of that reality, our feelings are often contingent upon momentary circumstances or fleeting desires. We're excited when things fall into place. We're frustrated when people disappoint us. We feel elated when others express their love for us. We feel crushed when relationships fail. Our emotions fluctuate from day to day—even from moment to moment!

This is not the case with God. His emotions don't waver depending on the circumstances. God's character is flawless, perfect, without blemish, complete, lacking nothing. He is not surprised by our failures or disconcerted by our weaknesses. He is steady, trustworthy, and unchanging. And His Word is clear about how He feels toward those who belong to Him.

Yahweh your God is among you, a warrior who saves. He will rejoice over you with gladness. He will bring you quietness with His love. He will delight in you with shouts of joy. —Zephaniah 3:17

The LORD values those who fear Him, those who put their hope in His faithful love. —Psalm 147:11

Your eyes saw me when I was formless; all my days were written in Your book and planned before a single one of them began. —Psalm 139:16

How great is Your goodness that You have stored up for those who fear You and accomplished in the sight of everyone for those who take refuge in You. —Psalm 31:19

The eyes of the LORD are on the righteous, and His ears are open to their cry for help. —Psalm 34:15

"Because he loves me," says the LORD, "I will rescue him; I will protect him, for he acknowledges my name. He will call on me, and I will answer him; I will be with him in trouble, I will deliver him and honor him. With long life I will satisfy him and show him my salvation." —Psalm 91:14–16 NIV

Because of the LORD's faithful love we do not perish, for His mercies never end. They are new every morning; great is Your faithfulness! —Lamentations 3:22–23

*Do not fear, for I am with you; do not be afraid, for I am your God. I will strengthen you; I will help you; I will hold on to you with My righteous right hand.* —Isaiah 41:10

*Look! God's dwelling is with humanity, and He will live with them. They will be His people, and God Himself will be with them and be their God. He will wipe away every tear from their eyes. Death will no longer exist: grief, crying, and pain will exist no longer, because the previous things have passed away.* —Revelation 21:3–4

Think about the words you've just read. What do these verses teach you about God's character? What do they say about His feelings toward those who belong to Him? You are beautiful and precious to the One who created you. He knows you completely and loves you perfectly. Choose to let how God feels about you shape the way you feel about yourself.

*Q.* **What does God think about you?**

**Scan for Video Answers!**

# *Survey*

## LIFE WITH NO REGRETS

*by Vicki Courtney*

Call me weird, but I like to read obituaries. My family makes fun of me, but I find it fascinating to read about people who have passed on. It's pretty humbling when you stop and think that our lives will someday be summed up in a few brief paragraphs at our funerals or in an online obituary. One guy I read about had a family member who said, "He wanted to live life with no regrets and he did just that." Hmm . . . That one sentence really got me thinking. Is it really possible to live life without a single regret? I don't think so. Surely this guy at some point in his life said an unkind word to someone. I'm pretty sure he lied, cheated, or lusted in his heart. No one is perfect, so we know he committed sins. Did he not regret them? Did he not regret when his actions hurt others? Maybe I'm overanalyzing this, but I don't think I can admire someone who "lives life with no regrets."

Some of the biggest regrets of my life came during my high school and college years. "If I could go back and do it over again . . ." Have you ever heard someone say that? Probably so. In life we will make mistakes. Some people will make more than others, but we will all make them. It seems to me that the key is to live with as few regrets as possible. That means learning from the mistakes we make, then moving on. Philippians 3:13–14 says, "Brothers and sisters, I do not consider myself yet to have taken hold of it. But one thing I do: Forgetting what is behind and straining toward what is ahead, I press on toward the goal to win the prize for which God has called me heavenward in Christ Jesus" (NIV). Sounds to me like a good remedy for regrets: forgetting what is behind and reaching forward to what is ahead.

## What about you? What's your biggest regret?

### Liz, 15

Telling a girl a secret and finding out she wasn't a real friend.

### Natalie, 12

My mom and I were in a coffee shop, and they were handing out free ice cream. There was only one left and I took it. Then I realized that a homeless man was about to take it. I kept it anyway, and later I felt so bad. I ended up throwing it up.

### Melissa, 14

My biggest regret would have to be talking behind my friend's back more than once.

### Heather, 17

Having sex before marriage!

### Kristin, 16

My biggest regret is not talking to two girls on my cheer team our freshman year.

### Kristen, 15

That I have anorexia.

### Kirsten, 13

Getting drunk at a party.

### Amanda, 18

I have two: Not waiting until marriage. Not getting rid of my ex-boyfriend sooner!

### Hannah, 16

When I go to church camp, learn so much, then I come home and I don't change anything. Basically I just have a camp high.

### Mary, 15

Not spending enough "quality time" with people and not having enough heart-to-heart talks with my sis. She's leaving for college this summer, and I'm just starting to realize all the stuff we never did.

### Becky, 15

My biggest regret is that I haven't spent enough time with my grandparents, who are starting to show their age.

### Hannah, 12

I always judge people. I want to stop, but sometimes words just slip out.

### Amber, 14

Being mad at my dad and then he died unexpectedly. I didn't get to tell him I loved him.

### Julie, 14

My biggest regret is probably giving a big piece of my heart emotionally to a guy who amazed me because he was such a godly guy, but who was still pretty immature—which I should have expected since he's only in high school! God knew what He was doing when He designed relationships for later in life!

### Amberly, 16

One of my biggest regrets is not trying hard enough in school. I don't make bad grades. I just know that I could do better.

### Becca, 16

Losing my parents' trust by lying.

### Amber, 19

Hanging out and being involved with people who drink and do bad things.

### Kaitlyn, 13

My regret is a regret but also a blessing from God. Last year I thought about killing myself. I decided I would starve myself, and I began to do so. A friend convinced me to stop, and since then I've been able to look back at that time and say to myself, *If God can get me through that, He can get me through anything.*

# Shame on Me, Again

*by Vicki Courtney*

It happened suddenly and without warning.

One minute I'm sitting in a booth, laughing over a cup of coffee with my youngest son on his college campus (which happens to be my alma mater). The next minute I'm driving away from my old college stomping grounds, and the mere sight of a corner drugstore triggers a painful reminder of my past.

It was the same corner drugstore that one of my roommates and I ducked into late one night under a cloak of darkness to purchase a pregnancy test. She was late and had assumed the worst. The test turned out negative, but it just as easily could have been me purchasing the test.

In fact, at age seventeen, it *had* been me—which is what triggered my sudden feelings of shame that day. Back then I was the one taking a pregnancy test, only my results were positive. This led to my decision to terminate the pregnancy. I've spoken openly about this part of my past and have been walking in victory for many years, but every so often, the feelings of shame still come.

And that's what shame does. It shows up uninvited to steal your joy and accuse your soul.

Dictionary.com defines shame as "the painful feeling arising from the consciousness of something dishonorable, improper, ridiculous, etc., done by oneself or another."

We avoid talking about shame because it is messy.

We see the earliest account of shame in the immediate aftermath of Adam and Eve's sin in the garden (Genesis 3). Prior to their sin, Scripture tells us they were both naked and unashamed. One chapter later they are sewing fig leaves together and playing a game of hide-and-seek with God. With that one forbidden bite came our first bitter taste of shame. Like Adam and Eve, our human instinct is to hide our shame. We attempt to cover it with modern-day fig leaves, ranging from addictions to breakneck busyness. We bury our shame beneath perfectionism, good deeds, and yes, even ministry service. Been there. Done that.

Some people are more prone to experiencing feelings of shame, while others seem better equipped to avoid its sting with a healthy understanding of guilt and grace. Those who grew up in households where shame was a mainstay of the family diet will often turn around and serve it to their own families, passing it down from generation to generation.

Shame is not the same as guilt. Guilt says, "What you did was bad." Shame says, "What you did was bad. Therefore, you are a bad person."

Shame is not the same as regret. Regret says, "If I could go back and do things differently, I'd do this . . . or that." Shame says, "I'll never get it right. I'm a failure."

Shame is not the same as embarrassment. Embarrassment says, "Everyone experiences embarrassing moments." Shame says, "I'm a loser, and nothing will change that fact."

Guilt is always connected to behavior, while shame is always connected to identity. Guilt draws us toward God, but shame sends us away from God.

We can't completely abolish painful reminders of shame that show up uninvited on the doorsteps of our souls, but we can refuse to answer the door. And that's exactly what I did that day as I drove past the drugstore. When the old shame tapes began to play, I hit the Eject button and boldly declared out loud this truth: "Therefore, there is now no condemnation for those who are in Christ Jesus" (Romans 8:1 NIV). Over and over I proclaimed it, until once again I believed it. I showed shame the door. And you can too.

# Jesus Changes Everything

*by Ali Claxton*

She could feel the stares as she walked through town. In their eyes she was beyond hope, past the point of redemption, too broken to ever belong. She felt worthless, and the weight of her shame had become unbearably heavy.

She desperately wanted to avoid the whispers, so she headed to the well in the heat of the day when no one else dared to face the blaring sun. As she walked, she couldn't help but think how pointless this ritual seemed. She would fill up her jug with water and carry it home, but soon enough it would be empty, and she would do this all over again.

Day after day, the struggle to find meaning and fulfillment taunted her. She'd found a temporary sense of belonging in romantic relationships, but she knew the excitement would fade and her affection would shift to someone new. She had held out hope that one day she'd discover a love that could heal her heart and satisfy her soul. After years of dreaming, she now doubted such a love existed.

It was quiet when she arrived. The only one near the well was a Jewish man she didn't recognize. She kept her eyes down, knowing He wouldn't acknowledge her existence. Jews didn't associate with Samaritans, so His request startled her. She felt unnerved and intrigued at the same time. She couldn't quite make sense of the situation. Why would He ask her for water? He had to know the risks of speaking to a Samaritan woman—especially one like her.

She responded to His request, asking, "How is it that you, a Jew, ask for a drink from me, a woman of Samaria?" (John 4:9 ESV). He answered by saying, "If you knew the gift of God, and who it is that is saying to you, 'Give me a drink,' you would have asked him, and he would have given you living water" (v. 10 ESV).

What a strange thing to say. She looked at the well, knowing from past experience there was nothing miraculous about the water she had drawn from it. She asked the man where this "living water" could be found.

His response stirred something deep within her. His words were confident, yet spoken with a gentleness that held her attention: "Everyone who drinks of this water will be thirsty again, but whoever drinks of the water that I will give him will never be thirsty again. The water that I will give him will become in him a spring of water welling up to eternal life" (John 4:13–14 ESV).

She was still unsure where the conversation was going, but He had her full attention now. Could there be such a thing as living water? How could a well never run dry? With questions swirling in her mind, she wondered what He would say if she asked for some of this water. Would He laugh at her? Would He walk away? Surely if He knew her reputation, He would have already parted company with her.

As soon as the words came out of her mouth, she felt a spark of hope flickering inside her. If she could just get some of the living water He spoke of, then she would never have to walk this lonely path again. His response came quickly, and with His words her hope faded. He wanted her to go and get her husband. She dropped her gaze to the ground, unable to hide her shame. There was no point in lying to Him. What good would it do? She would tell Him that she had no husband, then simply walk away. He didn't need to hear all the gory details of her tainted love life. The fact that she'd been married five times and the man she was with now wasn't her husband seemed too scandalous to say out loud.

She heard no condemnation in His voice. He pulled back the curtain of her life and uncovered her shame. How in the world did He know about her failed marriages or about the man she now lived with? He must be a prophet. But as the dialogue unfolded, she became more aware that she was standing in the presence of One greater than a prophet. This man who offered living water was the Messiah they'd been waiting for. The only One with the power to save stood before her with grace in His eyes. He was the source of the love she so desperately longed for—a love that could heal, forgive, redeem, and carry away her shame. She had come to the well a broken woman, but her encounter with Jesus changed everything.

The story in John 4 is a beautiful picture of grace. We may not share the same pattern of sin that plagued the Samaritan woman's life, but we all stand before God guilty and broken. We know the weight of shame— we all have mistakes in our past that threaten to crush us and make us feel unworthy. We have all run to other sources trying to find what only Jesus can provide. Living water. Infinite grace. Eternal life. Only He has the power to forgive and heal us.

Your worth is not defined by your past. Once you encounter Jesus, you are made new. His grace changes everything!

*Everyone who drinks of this water will be thirsty again, but whoever drinks of the water that I will give him will never be thirsty again.*
—John 4:13 ESV

# ARE YOU THIRSTY FOR MORE?

*by Ashley Anderson*

You, God, are my God, earnestly I
seek you; I thirst for you, my whole
being longs for you, in a dry and
parched land where there is no water.
—Psalm 63:1 NIV

I'm not sure exactly where you are in your faith. Maybe you are hearing God's voice for the first time and it's exciting. Maybe it's been awhile since you've talked to Him, and you're worried He's angry with you. Maybe you love God but the worries, busyness, and struggles of life have blocked your view of Him. Maybe you're sensing that He is telling you to take a step of faith, but you're not sure what to do.

Wherever you are, I know that much like David (who wrote Psalm 63), we all can feel desperate for something more than what we are experiencing in our lives. Even as Christians we sometimes wonder, *Is this really it? Or is there something more to life that I'm missing?*

As we try to answer those nagging questions, we franticly search for something to quench our thirst. Anything.

In the book of Jeremiah, God warns the Israelites that they have done just that: "My people have committed two sins: They have forsaken me, the spring of living water, and have dug their own cisterns, broken cisterns that cannot hold water" (2:13).

God says that His people often make two big mistakes when we are thirsty:

**Mistake #1: We walk away from the true living water.** God is not talking about real $H_2O$ here; He is talking about Himself. Jesus called Himself living water that will forever quench our thirst as long as we come to Him (John 7:37–38). And we *know* this is true! We have experienced Jesus and all He has to offer; yet we still turn away from Him.

**Mistake #2: We create broken cisterns for ourselves.** A cistern is like a water tank. We turn away from Jesus, the living water, and build our own water tanks. But there's another problem: The cisterns we have built are broken. In fact, they are downright disgusting. They're cracked, all the water has leaked out, and there's nothing left but muddy sludge. And what does God say we do? We are so thirsty that we get down on our hands and knees and try to slurp some dirty water from the sludge. Mmmm . . . sounds good, huh?

When I was in high school, cheerleading was my thing. Our squad was very competitive, and it quickly became a huge part of my identity. My junior year I was trying out for the varsity squad, and I was the front-runner for squad captain. The week of tryouts I got deathly sick—probably because I was so stressed out. The morning of the tryout I had a 102-degree fever. When it was my turn to perform, I entered the gym and saw three judges sitting behind their intimidating little table. As soon as I was given the cue to begin, I started my running tumbling pass and—*snap!* I broke my arm. I stood up, looked at the judges, grabbed my arm, and started weeping.

The principal who was overseeing the tryout led me back to the locker room. I confidently told him that I would need a few minutes to pull myself together, then I was planning to finish the tryout—with a broken arm. He looked at me like I had lost my mind. I went back to the gym and completed the entire tryout with a swollen, broken arm. I'm not sure if the judges had sympathy for me or if they were scared of what I might do if I didn't make the team—but either way, I was a varsity cheerleader the next year.

I think it's safe to say that cheerleading was a big cistern I had built, and I was not willing to let go of it easily. In my mind I didn't know who I would be apart from cheerleading, so I was desperate to slurp up the muddy water, even though I could hear a stream of living water flowing not too far away. After I graduated and went to college—where I was no longer a cheerleader—I was forced to realize that cheerleading truly was a broken cistern. It was a temporary and poor solution to the thirst I was feeling in my life.

Here are few of my other cisterns and an example of when I know they are broken:

| Cisterns | When I know they are broken |
|---|---|
| My favorite food or coffee | When the enjoyment fades |
| Checking off my to-do list | When I can't get it all done |
| Long convo with my best friend | When she doesn't say the right thing |
| A text from the guy in my life | When one compliment isn't enough |
| A new outfit | When I still obsess over my body |
| My Christian activities | When I feel like a fake because I feel far from God |
| My popular Instagram post | When I watch others get *way* more likes than me |

Obviously, some of these "cisterns" are good things! I'm not saying we should never buy a new outfit, or have a friend, or a boyfriend, or accomplish something great, or try out for the cheerleading squad. The point is that we rely too much on these things for our fulfillment.

*And all the while, God is saying . . .*
*Come to Me!*
*Listen to Me!*
*Let Me be your living water!*
*Let Me satisfy you!*
*Let Me fill you up!*
*Let Me quench your thirst!*

# WISE WORDS FROM COLLEGE GIRLS

*by Ashley Anderson*

We asked a group of college girls to share some verses of Scripture they clung to for hope and encouragement at your age . . .

### Lezli, 21

"You are altogether beautiful, my darling; there is no flaw in you."
—Song of Songs 4:7 NIV

### Charli, 20

"She is clothed with strength and dignity; she can laugh at the days to come."
—Proverbs 31:25 NIV

### Jenna, 22

"I praise you because I am fearfully and wonderfully made; your works are wonderful, I know that full well."—Psalm 139:14 NIV

### Janie, 20

"I have told you these things, so that in me you may have peace. In this world you will have trouble. But take heart! I have overcome the world."
—John 16:33 NIV

### Alison, 21

"The grass withers and the flowers fall, but the word of our God endures forever."—Isaiah 40:8 NIV

### Katie, 20

"Fixing our eyes on Jesus, the pioneer and perfecter of faith. For the joy set before him he endured the cross, scorning its shame, and sat down at the right hand of the throne of God.—Hebrews 12:2 NIV

### Joelle, 21

"Charm is deceptive, and beauty is fleeting; but a woman who fears the LORD is to be praised."—Proverbs 31:30 NIV

### Amanda, 20

"The Lord your God is with you, the Mighty Warrior who saves. He will take great delight in you; in his love he will no longer rebuke you, but will rejoice over you with singing."—Zephaniah 3:17 NIV

### Caroline, 21

"Be strong and courageous. Do not be afraid or terrified because of them, for the LORD your God goes with you; he will never leave you nor forsake you." —Deuteronomy 31:6 NIV

### Carly, 22

"Now faith is confidence in what we hope for and assurance about what we do not see."—Hebrews 11:1 NIV

### Hannah, 22

"And a voice from heaven said, 'This is my Son, whom I love; with him I am well pleased.'"—Matthew 3:17 NIV

### Taylor, 21

"'For I know the plans I have for you,' declares the LORD, 'plans to prosper you and not to harm you, plans to give you hope and a future.'"—Jeremiah 29:11 NIV

### Bailey, 22

"'Though the mountains be shaken and the hills be removed, yet my unfailing love for you will not be shaken nor my covenant of peace be removed,' says the LORD, who has compassion on you."—Isaiah 54:10 NIV

# The Beautiful Truth

*by Ali Claxton*

When was the last time the sight of something beautiful took your breath away? Maybe you were looking out over the ocean at sunset, mesmerized by the colors colliding across the horizon. Or looking up at the night sky as brilliant specks of light crowded the expanse as far as your eyes could see. Or maybe it wasn't the scenery at all. Maybe it was a moment when you were surrounded by people you love, who filled you with an overwhelming sense of belonging.

These experiences remind us that beauty is more than what we see with our eyes; it's something we embrace with our hearts. We long for beauty. We want to see it, hear it, and feel it because the presence of beauty points to a much deeper reality. You see, the One who spoke the world into being and breathed life into every living thing has woven glimpses of His glory into all of creation. We may have different criteria for what is pleasing to the eye or compelling to the heart, but when we look at life through the lens of eternity, we recognize that there is beauty all around us.

Do you struggle to see beauty in yourself? In others? How about in your circumstances? How you answer these questions is significant because it shapes the way you see the world. Beauty denotes value and worth, but not in the shallow way the world claims. Despite what television ads and billboards display, being beautiful doesn't mean we airbrush our scars and hide everything that falls short of perfection. In fact, we can never fully appreciate beauty until we see our brokenness and embrace the One who makes us new. And we will never fully appreciate our worth until we come to know the One who calls us His own.

Because real beauty goes much deeper than appearance-level, it's easy to overlook. If our perspective is based only on what we can see with our eyes, we cannot recognize it. With every failure or rejection, we'll be tempted to see ourselves as less valuable. With every conflict or betrayal, it will become far more difficult to see the good in others. With every trial we encounter, we'll struggle to see God's hand at work, restoring and redeeming our circumstances. But we can always find beauty when we search for it—when we choose to look past the surface and let our hearts embrace what our eyes can't see.

One of my favorite verses in Scripture is Ecclesiastes 3:11 because it reminds me where beauty begins and ends: "He has made everything beautiful in its time" (NIV).

The Creator of the universe invites us to celebrate the beauty of His creation, to see reflections of His radiance in people, in places, and even in our circumstances. Our Creator is the One who defines what is beautiful and the One who deserves the praise when we recognize His handiwork. When we look at the mountains or admire a delicate flower, we should marvel at the intricate work of His artistry. When we look at people, we should celebrate their worth simply because they were made in His image. When we look at ourselves, we should see His purposeful design reflected in our character and countenance. And when we consider our circumstances, even our most difficult times can show us the depths of His love for us. This is beauty the way God intended.

*He has made everything beautiful in its time.*

*—Ecclesiastes 3:11*

# A Letter from God

*by Ashley Anderson*

My beloved child,

I know everything about you. I know all of your habits and little idiosyncrasies (Psalm 139:3). I wanted you to resemble Me (Genesis 1:27), so I formed you with My very hands—your body, face, mind, emotions, and personality. When you were still in your mother's womb, I knew exactly who you would be (Psalm 139:13). I was there when you were born, and you were beautiful (Psalm 22:10; Song of Songs 4:7). Before your parents even chose a name for you, I had already called you Mine (Isaiah 43:1). And now, every day I am right there with you, walking ahead of you and protecting you. You are never out of My sight. I even know what you will say before you say it (Psalm 139:3–10).

The truth is that you have stolen My heart (Song of Songs 4:9), and therefore I have created so much to make you happy—relationships, food, mountains, oceans, sunsets, animals, birds, trees, and flowers (Genesis 1:28–29). I think you are absolutely lovely and are becoming lovelier each day you grow closer to Me (Song of Songs 2:14).

When you asked for My forgiveness through Christ, I forgave you once and for all; and I will never hold anything against you (Psalm 32:1–2). Even now there is nothing you could ever do to make Me stop loving you (Ephesians 2:4–5). You are whiter than snow in my eyes (Psalm 51:7). Even your most shameful mistakes do not scare Me or make Me want to pull away from you (Romans 8:1). In fact, it's the opposite. Every time you turn away from Me, I am waiting for you with open arms (Luke 15:22–24). Don't believe Satan's lies—I am not angry with you. My heart is a fountain overflowing with grace and compassion that never runs dry. And, My mercies are new every morning (Lamentations 3:22–23).

This world is a difficult place, and I don't want you to walk through it without Me. There are few things that are stable in life, but I will never change. I am the same yesterday, today, and forever (Hebrews 13:8). The world will lie to you, but I want you to know that I will always tell you the truth (Romans 3:4) because I am the truth (John 14:6). Your family and friends may forget you, but I will never forget you. How could I? I have engraved you on the palms of My hands (Isaiah 49:15–16). When you feel like things can't get any worse, I will be there (Psalm 30:3). When you're weak, I'll be strong (2 Corinthians 12:10). I will carry you in My arms if I have to, so that you can be as close to

Me as possible (Isaiah 40:11). You can count on Me to fight for you (Psalm 18:35; 146:6–9). When you are in pain, I will comfort you and turn your sadness into joy (Jeremiah 31:13). And don't lose hope, because a day is coming when there will be no more crying or pain (Revelation 21:4).

When you are exhausted, I'll give you physical rest and rest for your soul (Psalm 127:2; Matthew 11:29). When you are feeling overwhelmed, I will be with you (Isaiah 43:2). I will never leave you (Matthew 28:20), and I will be faithful to you until the end (1 Corinthians 1:9).

I have so many dreams for your life. I want to satisfy you when you realize that this world is not enough (Jeremiah 31:25). I want to liberate you from all your fears (Psalm 34:4). I want to heal all your deepest wounds (Matthew 9:22). I want to make you stronger than you realize you can be (Psalm 29:11) and give you a supernatural peace that the world will not understand (Philippians 4:7). I want you to have abundant life every day through the same Spirit who raised Jesus from the dead and now lives inside of you (Romans 8:11; John 10:10). I want you to learn and develop the gifts I have given you and use them for My glory (1 Corinthians 1:7).

If you trust me, I promise you these things: The more you get to know Me, the more you will understand yourself (Ephesians 1:11–12). If you make our relationship your treasure, then I will give you the desires of your heart (Psalm 37:4). With Me you have nothing to fear (Isaiah 41:13). Every time you trust in Me, you will not regret it (Romans 10:11). Your future is in My hands, and it's going to be amazing. Your dreams cannot contain the dreams I have for you. You can't begin to imagine the adventure that awaits (Jeremiah 29:11).

My love for you knows no limits,

### God, your Father

*Q. What beautiful dreams does God have for you?*

Scan for Video Answers!

# Fixer-Upper

*by Pam Gibbs*

Home improvement shows have taken over television. If you channel surf, you'll come across shows that feature yard transformations, loving it or listing it, basement do-overs, living room face-lifts, and "flipping houses" all over the country. Some shows even feature a renovation of the entire house, from the attic to the subfloor. Nothing is left the same but the studs and frames.

Believe it or not, those extreme makeovers don't just happen with houses. They happen to people too. Not a makeup or wardrobe change, but a transformation of the heart. And Jesus is the architect and designer of that spiritual makeover.

## What You Once Were

Did you know that Scripture paints an unflattering picture of your life without Christ? Here are just a few of the descriptions. The book of Titus says, "At one time we too were foolish, disobedient, deceived and enslaved by all kinds of passions and pleasures. We lived in malice and envy, being hated and hating one another" (3:3 NIV). Second Timothy 3:2–4 describes nonbelievers as "lovers of themselves, lovers of money, boastful, proud, abusive, disobedient to parents, ungrateful, unholy, without love, unforgiving, slanderous, without self-control, brutal, not lovers of the good, treacherous, rash, conceited, lovers of pleasure rather than lovers of God" (NIV). Doesn't sound very good, does it?

## A New Creature

You may be thinking to yourself, *Hey! Wait a minute! Sometimes I disobey my parents. Sometimes I'm envious of my friends. Does that mean I'm not a Christian?* It depends on your relationship with Jesus. In 2 Corinthians 5:17, Paul says that if you give your life to Christ, you become a "new creation . . . the old has gone, the new is here!" (NIV). Just like a contractor gutting a house, the Holy Spirit comes in and begins to radically transform you. Notice that Paul didn't say that you are an improved version of you. God doesn't just do touch-ups here and there. A fresh coat of paint and some

new curtains won't do. He changes everything because every part of you needs changing. Sin affects every neuron, cell, and atom in you, spiritually speaking. That's why God is after your whole heart, not just pieces of it. The process of becoming more like Him, more like the person He created you to be, is called *sanctification*. Change began the instant you became a believer, and change will continue until you die or until Jesus comes back—whichever comes first.

## When the Pictures Look the Same

Here's the problem in today's culture: sometimes you can't tell if a person has given her life to Christ because her life looks just like it did before she became a Christian. Same habits, same dress, same attitudes, same cuss words, same behavior. And that's a big problem. When you aren't any different from your Buddhist friend or your atheist teammate, then one of two things is true. Either you have never really given your life to Christ, or you've bought into the lie that you can follow Jesus and still be like the world.

## A Work in Progress

Remember the analogy of the home makeovers? Every makeover show will feature one thing: before-and-after pictures. The pictures show what the old looked like in order to highlight the dramatic change that took place. Similarly, your life is a living before-and-after photo album of the work that Christ has done in your life. Only the changes won't be quite so noticeable. Little by little, as you spend more time with Him—through reading the Bible, praying, being at church, and spending time with other Christians—things will begin to change. Small things. You yell at your sister a little less. You are more kind to the kid who sits alone at school. You feel bad when you sin. (That's called the conviction of the Holy Spirit.) You want to read your Bible. All of those changes are snapshots, pictures of the progress that Christ is making in your life.

## I Surrender All

If you don't see any changes, then take a look at your heart. Has it grown cold toward Him? Are you rebelling against Him? Resisting the change He wants to make in your life? If so, you need to find out why. The Holy Spirit will work in you, but only if you are a willing participant. He won't work if you refuse His small nudges. Following Jesus is a daily choice to surrender yourself to Him again and again. Remember that the changes God wants to make in your life are for your good and His glory. And that's the best kind of makeover. Ever.

*Therefore, if anyone is in Christ, the new creation has come: The old has gone, the new is here! —2 Corinthians 5:17 NIV*

# MISTAKEN IDENTITY

*by Vicki Courtney*

It's the kind of news story that leaves you shaking your head in confusion. On December 17, 2012, the body of Timothy Henry Gray, age sixty, was found under the overpass of Union Pacific Railroad in Evanston, Wyoming. According to a coroner's report, the police found no signs of foul play and determined his cause of death was hypothermia.

But Gray wasn't your average transient. He was the adopted great-grandson of former US senator William Andrews Clark and the half great-nephew of the reclusive New York copper heiress Huguette Clark, who had died the year before at the age of 104 with an amassed $300 million fortune. Gray was among twenty great-nieces and great-nephews who each stood to inherit $19 million from their great-aunt's estate. Attorneys for the relatives had been searching for Gray in the weeks before his death. Not that the fortune would have likely made much difference. Family members had not seen Timothy Gray in over two decades, claiming he had "severe post-traumatic stress symptoms due to childhood traumas." A coroner reported that at the time of his death, a wallet was found on him, and it contained undeposited checks from a few years back, one of which was described as "large."

Timothy Gray's story is a desperately sad account of mistaken identity. Gray was an adopted heir who never realized his true worth. Instead, he chose to live as a homeless transient. You might be surprised to find we share something in common with Gray's story. We, too, are adopted heirs (Romans 8:17; Ephesians 1:5). Take a look at what Paul told the church at Galatia:

"But when the set time had fully come, God sent his Son, born of a woman, born under the law, to redeem those under the law, that we might receive adoption to sonship. Because you are his sons, God sent the Spirit of his Son into our hearts, the Spirit who calls out, '*Abba*, Father!' So you are no longer a slave, but God's child; and since you are his child, God has made you also an heir" (Galatians 4:4–7 NIV).

Allow the truth of these verses to sink into the core of your being. You. Me. Adopted. By the God of the universe. Free to call Him Daddy. In spite of this life-altering truth, many believers suffer from their own cases of mistaken identity, failing to ever accept their true worth and standing before God. No longer are we alienated from God. We've been adopted by the One who owns "the cattle on a thousand hills" (Psalm 50:10). Sadly, many of us will go to our graves as spiritual paupers, sitting on fortunes of unspent blessings and benefits from God's great storehouse of grace.

Take, for example, the mistaken identity many believers ascribe to themselves when they say they are a "sinner saved by grace." For the majority of my years as a believer, I have readily identified myself this way. While it is true that I will struggle with sin until I meet Jesus face-to-face, the truth is that sin no longer defines me. In fact, Scripture calls me (and you) a *saint*. Part of the reality of our transformation—old things have passed away, and new things have come—is the new identity we assumed on the day we became believers. Our old sinner-selves were crucified with Christ's death on the cross. Paul said it this way: "I have been crucified with Christ and I no longer live, but Christ lives in me. The life I now live in the body, I live by faith in the Son of God, who loved me and gave himself for me" (Galatians 2:20 NIV). Thanks to the finished work of Jesus Christ, we are sanctified and given a new identity as saints. Paul called believers "those sanctified in Christ Jesus and called to be his holy people, together with all those everywhere who call on the name of our Lord Jesus Christ" (1 Corinthians 1:2 NIV).

You may think I am being nitpicky when I state we are not just "sinners saved by grace." If we define ourselves primarily as "sinners," that title can act as a self-fulfilling prophecy. Author Steve McEvey said, "If you believe you are fundamentally a sinner, your default setting will be to act like a sinner. To behave in any other way would be to act inconsistently with the person you perceive yourself to be. After all, what do you expect a 'sinner' to do? *Sin*. Sinning is simply the normal behavior for a sinner."[1]

I remember a particular moment when the reality of who I am in Christ began to set me free. Until that moment, I had seen myself as "a sinner saved by grace." When I sinned, I would remind myself of God's grace, but my focus was on stopping the sinful behavior. Because it is our nature to sin, I felt like I was caught in a never-ending battle when I would sin yet again. I was trying to live as a "saved sinner"—which is a contradictory identity. I was simply living up to my own low expectations. Even if I could overcome one area of sin, another temptation was always waiting in the wings to trip me up. It was exhausting. It certainly didn't feel like the victorious life I had read about in the Bible, and I felt anything but free.

Saddest of all, this brand of Christianity began to feel like nothing more than a regimen of behavior in which the end-goal was perfection. My walk had been reduced to a sin-management program, not a growing relationship with the One who set me free. I looked for the right formula of spiritual disciplines, rules, accountability, and anything I could find to combat the sinner within.

As a disclaimer, I am not suggesting these things won't help thwart sinful actions. My point is simply this: alone, apart from the power of Christ and apart from our true identity as saints, spiritual disciplines just won't do the trick. Charles Spurgeon once said, "I have found, in my own spiritual life, that the more rules I lay down for myself, the more sins I commit."[2] In Colossians 2:20–23, Paul warned of relying solely on self-imposed regulations, saying, "They lack any value in restraining sensual indulgence" (v. 23 NIV). No matter how hard we try, rules and regulations won't kill our sinful appetites because rules feed our flesh. Without God's power, rules are futile at stopping sin.

For me, the transforming moment came when I found myself standing at a crossroads of a temptation—again. I had stumbled in that area before and I was on the verge of taking the same wrong path—again. I couldn't muster enough strength to choose the right path. I needed help. The Holy Spirit whispered a simple yet profound truth into my heart: "This is not who you are." The reality of what Christ had done flooded my heart. Just as Paul had said,

"I have been crucified with Christ" (Galatians 2:20 NIV), I, too, could say the same. Old, pre-saved, sinner Vicki had been crucified; and in her place was a new creation. When Christ was resurrected, with Him came my new identity. I was transformed from a sinner to a saint. His goal in saving me was not only to forgive my sins, but also to leave me with the power to be alive in Him—a resurrection power to overcome sin.

In his book *The Practice of the Presence of God*, Brother Lawrence said, "I regard myself as the most wretched of all men, stinking and covered with sores, and as one who has committed all sorts of crimes against his King. Overcome by remorse, I confess all my wickedness to Him, ask His pardon and abandon myself entirely to Him to do with as He will. But this King, filled with goodness and mercy, far from chastising me, lovingly embraces me, makes me eat at His table, serves me with His own hands, gives me the keys of His treasures and treats me as His favorite. He talks with me and is delighted with me in a thousand and one ways; He forgives me and relieves me of my principle bad habits without talking about them; I beg Him to make me according to His heart and always the more weak and despicable I see myself to be, the more beloved I am of God."[3]

Do you see yourself in a similar light? My turning point came when I was overwhelmed by a deep understanding of what Christ had done. Filled with goodness and mercy, He met me in my mess and reminded me of my true identity as a saint. As a result, I want to live up to my new identity—one I don't deserve but have been given with God's gift of mercy and grace. Christ overcame the grave, and with that same power, I, too, can overcome sin and temptation and live a victorious life. I am free!

Oh, sure, I still stumble and fall from time to time, but I get up and remind myself, *This is not who I am*. Saints are not chained to their sin. Saints have the power to overcome sin. Saints walk in freedom. I'm a saint, and, therefore, I want to behave like a saint, not a sinner.

What is your identity? A sinner saved by grace, or a saint who still sins? Mercy has declared you a saint, and Jesus is waiting to set you free.

### Sources:

1. Steve McEvey, *52 Lies Head in Church Every Sunday: And Why the Truth Is So Much Better* (Eugene, OR: Harvest House, 2011), 13.

2. Charles Spurgeon, quoted in Warren Wiersbe, *Wycliffe Handbook of Preaching and Preachers* (Chicago, IL: Moody Press, 1984), 235.

3. Brother Lawrence, *The Brother Lawrence Collection* (Radford, VA: Wilder Publications, 2008), 24.

# Who Are You?

*by Ali Claxton*

We all want to believe we have value, that we add something beautiful to this world. We want to wake up with confidence and walk through our days unhindered by labels and insecurities. We want to feel brave and extraordinary.

We want our lives to matter. But if we're being honest, most days we don't *feel* all that significant. We're unsure of ourselves more often than we care to admit. We can't see past our mistakes and weaknesses to the potential planted deep within us.

The struggle to find our true identity is a necessary part of life's journey. Where you choose to search for your sense of self-worth will make all the difference. You won't discover your infinite value in temporary things like appearance, achievements, or other people's opinions. You weren't meant to be validated by such a shortsighted view of worth. There is only one source that can show you who you are and who you're becoming. The only way to truly see yourself is to look through the lens of the God who created you.

And here's what He says about you . . .

### *You are beautiful:*

I will praise You because I have been remarkably and wonderfully made. Your works are wonderful, and I know this very well.

—Psalm 139:14

### *You are a new creation:*

Therefore, if anyone is in Christ, he is a new creation; old things have passed away, and look, new things have come.

—2 Corinthians 5:17

### *You are alive and free:*

But God, who is rich in mercy, because of His great love that He had for us, made us alive with the Messiah even though we were dead in trespasses. You are saved by grace!

—Ephesians 2:4–5

Therefore, if the Son sets you free, you really will be free.

—John 8:36

### *You are a child of God:*

See what great love the Father has lavished on us, that we should be called children of God! And that is what we are!

—1 John 3:1

But to all who did receive Him, He gave them the right to be children of God, to those who believe in His name.

—John 1:12

### *You are forgiven:*

He has not dealt with us as our sins deserve or repaid us according to our offenses. For as high as the heavens are above the earth, so great is His faithful love toward those who fear Him. As far as the east is from the west, so far has He removed our transgressions from us. As a father has compassion on his children, so the Lord has compassion on those who fear Him.

—Psalm 103:10–13

Therefore, no condemnation now exists for those in Christ Jesus, because the Spirit's law of life in Christ Jesus has set you free from the law of sin and of death.

—Romans 8:1–2

### *You are victorious:*

You are from God, little children, and you have conquered them, because the One who is in you is greater than the one who is in the world.

—1 John 4:4

### *You are a friend of God:*

I do not call you slaves anymore, because a slave doesn't know what his master is doing. I have called you friends, because I have made known to you everything I have heard from My Father.

—John 15:15

### *You are a child of light:*

You are all children of the light and children of the day. We do not belong to the night or to the darkness.

—1 Thessalonians 5:5

### *You are a citizen of heaven:*

But our citizenship is in heaven, from which we also eagerly wait for a Savior, the Lord Jesus Christ.

—Philippians 3:20

### *You are an ambassador for Christ:*

Therefore, we are ambassadors for Christ, certain that God is appealing through us. We plead on Christ's behalf, "Be reconciled to God."

—2 Corinthians 5:20

God's Word paints a beautiful picture of your identity. His truth defines you. Let His words sink deep into your heart and give you the confidence to be who you are.

# Too Busy for God?

*by Whitney Prosperi*

Have you ever noticed that it's cool to have a lot going on? I mean, when someone asks you what you've been doing, you don't want to say you've been watching the Weather Channel trying to understand barometric pressure or learning how to tweeze your eyebrows. You want to have something to say. Everyone seems to want to have lots going on. Maybe we use busyness to help us feel valued, or maybe it's just the by-product of too many options. It's just hard to say no when there are so many wonderful things to say yes to.

Whatever the case may be, if we're too busy for God, we're just too busy. Period. If you find yourself in this situation, read on. You'll find some helpful ways to make time for God in spite of a busy day or a busy life.

## *Make time with God a priority.*

You've probably heard it said that we find time for what we really care about. You probably take the time to brush your hair and get ready each morning. Most likely you give some attention to responding to important calls or text messages. And you don't miss out on important conversations with that some-one special when he calls or stops by. So why is it that time with God is often the last thing on our list? We do it if we find extra time, but when other things come up, it's usually the first thing to go.

Could it be that we know God will forgive us? I mean, that's His specialty, right? We can't always be assured our teacher will forgive us if we're late or that a friend will overlook an unreturned call. So we take advantage of His forgiveness, knowing that He'll be waiting for us the next time.

But why not make time with God our top priority? That way, other things may not get done or other people may not hear back from us, but God will. We just determine that time with Him is the last thing we toss out on a busy day. If you're willing to make that commitment, stop right now and pray. Ask Him to help you commit to spending time with Him each day, whether it is first thing in the morning, right after school, or before bed.

## *Say no to something else.*

While it's not popular to say no to opportunities that come up, sometimes we just have to if we're going to make time with God our top priority. Maybe you're involved in something that takes so much of your time that you're unable to keep your commitment to spend time alone with God. It could be a particular extracurricular activity or interest. If this is the case, consider cutting back time spent on this activity. Or you might even want to take a break from it altogether. You can always get involved in that activity later. The world won't end. I promise. And you might even find that you enjoy having a little free time to explore other interests.

Or maybe you are involved in a relationship that takes so much of your time that it's hard for you to squeeze in time with God. Here's a radical thought: Why not turn down the intensity of your relationship? If the other person doesn't understand, then that reveals a lot about him. Maybe you don't need to be pouring all of your time into that relationship anyway.

When I was in high school, a friend of mine decided that she was going to give up dating for a season so she could focus more on her relationship with God.

You may not want to do this, or you may be thinking you wish you had a dating life to take a break from; but maybe there's something else you want to eliminate so you can spend more time with God. It could be time spent on the computer, watching TV, or shopping. Saying no to something else will mean that you can say yes to the very best of all—Jesus.

You probably remember the story of Mary and Martha in the Bible. Martha was very busy. She would have fit in beautifully in our culture. But Mary chose to spend time with Jesus. She knew what was most important. She remembered what would matter in the course of forever. Jesus corrected Martha but praised Mary for her choices. Luke 10:41–42 says, "'Martha, Martha,' the Lord answered, 'you are worried and upset about many things, but few things are needed—or indeed only one. Mary has chosen what is better, and it will not be taken away from her'" (NIV).

Which person do you identify with more? Will you choose the many things that really don't make a difference, or the one thing that is absolutely critical? Make the right choice like Mary—and you won't regret it. Ever.

## Schedule time with God.

If you're going to be consistent in spending time with God, you have to set aside the time each day to do it. Make an appointment with God. It might be in the morning or the evening. It could be during lunch or right after school. What works best for you? For many the morning is the best time to spend with God. Before the day begins with all of its distractions and temptations, you can focus on His Word and His perspective.

Psalm 143:8 says, "Let me experience Your faithful love in the morning, for I trust in You. Reveal to me the way I should go because I long for You."

## Ask a friend for help.

Have you ever noticed that we have an easier time keeping our commitment when we know someone else has made the same one? I used to work out with a friend every morning at six. Now, you can bet I wouldn't have dragged myself out of bed if I didn't know she was waiting for me. Having this friend to hold me accountable helped me keep my commitment to getting in shape.

It's the same way in our relationship with God. If you know you want to get up each morning for time alone with God, but also know you could qualify as an Olympic medalist in pushing the snooze button, ask a friend to help you.

She doesn't have to come to your house and kick you out of bed. Just agree together to pray for one another, then ask each other how it's going.

### Don't be hard on yourself.

If you miss one day, don't throw in the towel. Just pick up the next day where you left off. Or find a few minutes later in the day to touch base with God. He isn't going to be mad or punish you. He's not asking you to be perfect. He wants you to get to know Him. Remember that this is a relationship. He is waiting to hear from you. Isaiah 30:18 says, "Therefore the LORD is waiting to show you mercy, and is rising up to show you compassion, for the LORD is a just God. All who wait patiently for Him are happy."

## Reflect . . .

1. Is spending time with God each day a priority in your life? Explain.

2. Is there an activity or a relationship that you need to step back from in order to have more time with God? If so, how are you going to take the first steps in doing this?

# Think This, Not That

*by Tami Overhauser*

When lies creep in and create doubt about your faith and the truth of Jesus, use the Word of God as your weapon. Replace those lies with these truths.

You will know the truth, and the truth will set you free. —John 8:32

Jesus told him, "I am the way, the truth, and the life. No one comes to the Father except through Me."—John 14:6

The LORD is near to all who call on him, to all who call on him in truth.—Psalm 145:18 NIV

Give thanks to the LORD, for He is good; His faithful love endures forever.—Psalm 107:1

Some trust in chariots and some in horses, but we trust in the name of the LORD our God.—Psalm 20:7 NIV

For you are saved by grace through faith, and this is not from yourselves; it is God's gift.—Ephesians 2:8

For everyone who calls on the name of the Lord will be saved. —Romans 10:13

Be still, and know that I am God.—Psalm 46:10 NIV

Therefore, if anyone is in Christ, he is a new creation; old things have passed away, and look, new things have come. —2 Corinthians 5:17

Do not fear, for I am with you; do not anxiously look about you, for I am your God. I will strengthen you, surely I will help you, surely I will uphold you with My righteous right hand. —Isaiah 41:10 NASB

But he said to me, "My grace is sufficient for you, for my power is made perfect in weakness." Therefore I will boast all the more gladly about my weaknesses, so that Christ's power may rest on me. —2 Corinthians 12:9 NIV

Be strong and courageous. Do not be afraid or terrified because of them, for the LORD your God goes with you; he will never leave you nor forsake you. —Deuteronomy 31:6

For I will forgive their wickedness and will remember their sins no more. —Hebrews 8:12 NIV

For I am convinced that neither death nor life, neither angels nor demons, neither the present nor the future, nor any powers, neither height nor depth, nor anything else in all creation, will be able to separate us from the love of God that is in Christ Jesus our Lord. —Romans 8:38–39 NIV

# The Truth About Forever

*by Vicki Courtney*

At some point in life, everyone wonders about eternity, about heaven and hell. Many teens mistakenly believe the popular opinion of today that says that heaven is open to pretty much everyone . . . except maybe really evil, wicked people. Of course, that begs the question: What constitutes *evil* or *wicked*? In other words, where is the cutoff between "good enough" and evil?

It only makes sense that the cutoff point is sin. And the truth is, only one sin will keep you out of heaven (and most importantly, separated from God). If you are starting to feel a bit short of breath, don't worry. God has provided a way for us to "make the cut" and spend eternity with Him.

As far as the opinion that heaven is open to most everyone, Matthew 7:13–14 makes it very clear when it says, "Enter through the narrow gate. For wide is the gate and broad is the road that leads to destruction, and many enter through it. But small is the gate and narrow the road that leads to life, and only a few find it" (NIV). If you're not sure if you are a Christian, carefully read below what it means to be a follower of Christ. Remember, this is the most important decision you will ever make in your life. Read carefully and try to understand what each verse means. Don't worry, we'll take it slowly, step-by-step.

## We learn about God's love in the Bible.

*For God so loved the world that he gave his one and only Son, that whoever believes in him shall not perish but have eternal life.— John 3:16 (NIV)*

God loves you. He wants to bless your life and make it happy, full, and complete. He wants to give you a life that will last forever, even after you die. *Perish* means to die and to be apart from God—forever. God wants you to have "eternal life" in heaven where you are with Him for eternity.

## We are sinful.

*For all have sinned and fall short of the glory of God.—Romans 3:23*

You may have heard someone say, "I'm only human—nobody's perfect." This Bible verse says the same thing: We are all sinners. No one is perfect. When we sin, we do things that are wrong—things that God would not agree with. The verse says we fall short of "God's glorious standard."

In order to meet God's standard, we would have to be perfect and stay that way . . . forever. Obviously, that's impossible since we are born sinners and we will continue to sin. But before you start to worry that you don't meet His standard, just wait. There's good news ahead.

## Sin has a penalty.

*For the wages [cost] of sin is death.* *—Romans 6:23 (NIV)*

Just as criminals must pay for their crimes, sinners must pay the penalty for their sins. Imagine this: What if every time we did something wrong, we had to pay a fine? Let's also say that our fine was not payable with money, but instead, was payable with our death. When we die, we will be separated from God for all eternity unless there is a way to pay for our sins. The Bible teaches that those who choose to be separated from God will spend eternity in a place called hell. You may have heard some bad things about hell, but the worst part about hell is that you are in a place where you never receive any of God's blessings, only His eternal punishment.

## Christ has paid the price for our sins!

*But God proves His own love for us in that while we were still sinners, Christ died for us!—Romans 5:8*

The Bible teaches that Jesus Christ, the sinless, perfect Son of God, has paid the price for all your sins. You may think you have to lead a good life and do good deeds before God will love you. It's good to do good deeds, but it won't pay the price for your sins and get you into heaven. The reason is that no matter how many good deeds you do, you still won't have a perfect score on life's test. But the Bible says that Christ loved you enough to die for you, even when you were acting unlovable. Pretty amazing, huh?!

## Salvation—eternity in heaven—is a free gift.

*For you are saved by grace through faith, and this is not from yourselves; it is God's gift—not from works, so that no one can boast.—Ephesians 2:8-9*

The word *grace* means a gift we don't deserve. It means Christ is offering to pay for something you could never pay for yourself: forgiveness of sins and eternal life. God's gift to you is free. You do not have to work for a gift—that's why it's called a gift. All you have to do is joyfully receive it. Believe with all your heart that Jesus Christ died for you and paid the price for your sins!

## Christ is at your heart's door.

*Here I am! I stand at the door and knock. If anyone hears my voice and opens the door, I will come in and eat with that person, and they with me.—Revelation 3:20 (NIV)*

Jesus Christ wants to have a personal relationship with you. He wants to be your very best friend. He wants you to talk to Him just like you would talk to your best friend. Picture, if you will, Jesus Christ standing at the door of your heart and knocking. Invite Him in; He is waiting for you to receive Him into your heart as Lord and Savior.

## You must receive Him.

*But to all who did receive Him, He gave them the right to be children of God.—John 1:12*

When you receive Christ into your heart, you become a child of God. You can talk to Him in prayer at any time about anything. The Christian life is a personal relationship with God through Jesus Christ, and best of all, it is a relationship that will last forever and ever. There is nothing you could ever do to make God stop loving you. Even though we will continue to sin, God still loves us. He never takes back His gift, so we don't have to worry about losing it. It is ours to keep forever.

So, what do you think about God's offer of forgiveness? Is this a gift you want to accept? If so, tell God. You don't have to say a fancy prayer—just talk to Him and tell Him that you believe that Jesus died on the cross for your sins and you want to receive that gift. That's all it takes! What are you waiting for? Stop and say a prayer right now.

Did you say a prayer and receive God's gift of forgiveness?

If you answered yes, you have an understanding of what it takes to spend eternity with God. Sometimes people say a quick little prayer but never change the course of their lives. They continue along the same path and bank on that little prayer as a sort of "fire insurance" to save them from hell. While it's not my place to say whether or not they are really Christians, I think we would all agree that if a sincere decision is made to follow Christ, a Christian's life will reflect it.

No, we won't be perfect. Even though Christ has paid the penalty for our sins, we will still blow it from time to time. Our lives should show some evidence of a changed heart. Someone who has made a sincere decision to follow Christ will feel convicted when they sin. They will seek to live a life that is pleasing to God. In the end, only you know if your decision to follow Christ is a sincere one. Your primary concern should not be getting to heaven so you can escape hell, but rather to live a life that is pleasing to Him today.

If you did not understand some of the verses above and you still aren't quite sure where you stand when it comes to God's gift of eternal life, please talk to someone who can help you better understand what it means to be a Christian. Maybe it's your parents, pastor, youth minister, mentor, or a relative. Maybe it's a friend's mom. Find someone who knows what it means to be a Christian and tell them you want to know more. This is the most important truth you will ever know. It will change the course of your life forever.

*(Above was adapted from "Your Christian Life" 1965, 1968, as "Aids to Christian Living," 1986 as "Practical Steps in Christian Living," 1995 as "Beginning Your Christian Life," 1997 as "Your Christian Life," Billy Graham Evangelistic Association.)*

But to all who did receive Him, He gave them the right to be children of God.
—John 1:12

**This is my prayer for you as you go forth and live out what you've learned:**

For this reason, since the day we heard about you, we have not stopped praying for you. We continually ask God to fill you with the knowledge of his will through all the wisdom and understanding that the Spirit gives, so that you may live a life worthy of the Lord and please him in every way: bearing fruit in every good work, growing in the knowledge of God, being strengthened with all power according to his glorious might so that you may have great endurance and patience, and giving joyful thanks to the Father, who has qualified you to share in the inheritance of his holy people in the kingdom of light. —Colossians 1:9–12 NIV

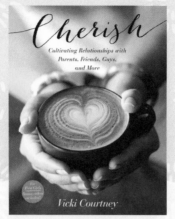